FIRST INVADERS

BELONGS TO

R.P. WELLAND

Z

OTHER BOOKS BY THE SAME AUTHOR

Intensive Care: A Memoir (Anvil Press, 2002)
Cuba: A Concise History for Travelers
(Penguin Books, 2002; Bluefield Books, 2000)
Twigg's Directory of 1001 BC Writers (Crown Publications, 1992)
Strong Voices: Conversations with 50 Canadian Writers (Harbour, 1988)
Vander Zalm, From Immigrant to Premier (Harbour, 1986)
Vancouver and Its Writers (Harbour, 1986)
Hubert Evans: The First Ninety-Three Years (Harbour, 1985)
For Openers: Conversations with 24 Canadian Writers (Harbour, 1981)

FIRST
INVADERS

The Literary Origins of British Columbia

ALAN TWIGG

RONSDALE

RONSDALE PRESS
3350 West 21st Avenue
Vancouver, B.C., Canada V6S 1G7
www.ronsdalepress.com

Typesetting: Get To The Point Graphics, in New Baskerville 11 pt on 14.1
Cover Design: David Lester & Alan Twigg
Paper: Ancient Forest Friendly Rolland "Enviro" – 100% post-consumer
         waste, totally chlorine-free and acid-free

Ronsdale Press wishes to thank the Canada Council for the Arts, the Government of
Canada through the Book Publishing Industry Development Program (BPIDP), and
the Province of British Columbia through the British Columbia Arts Council for their
support of its publishing program.

Library and Archives Canada Cataloguing in Publication

Twigg, Alan, 1952-
First invaders : the literary origins of British Columbia / Alan Twigg.

Includes bibliographical references.
ISBN 1-55380-018-4

1. British Columbia—Discovery and exploration—Early works to 1800.
2. Explorers—British Columbia—Biography—Early works to 1800.
3. British Columbia—History—Sources. I. Title.

FC3821.T84 2004   971.1'01   C2004-904954-2

At Ronsdale Press we are committed to protecting the environment. To this end we
are working with Markets Initiative (www.oldgrowthfree.com) and printers to phase
out our use of paper produced from ancient forests. This book is one step towards
that goal.

Printed in Canada by AGMV Marquis

To Ruby Twigg,
ninety-nine years young,
still fetching her firewood

*"One morning, very early, some of the men got up to go
hunting, and as they went outside the houses and looked over
the water, they saw something that they could not
understand.... They ran along the houses, calling to the rest
of the tribe, 'Come out and see what is in the water. It must be
a new island that has come in the night.'"*
—TSTASS-AYA (JENNY WYSE)
AS TOLD TO BERYL CRYER, CIRCA 1930;
NANAIMO MUSEUM

*Petroglyph depicts arrival of a European
ship near Nanaimo.*

*"The Indians didn't know what on earth it was when the ship
came into the harbour...so the Chief, Chief Maquinna, he sent
out his warriors.... So they went out to the ship and they
thought it was a fish come alive into people.... So they went
ashore and they told the big Chief: 'You know what we saw?
They've got white skin. But we're pretty sure that those people
on the floating thing, there, that they must have been fish.'"*
—WINIFRED DAVID
RECOUNTING NUU-CHAH-NULTH VERSION OF CAPTAIN COOK'S ARRIVAL
FROM *NU-TKA: CAPTAIN COOK AND THE SPANISH EXPLORERS
ON THE COAST*, SOUND HERITAGE, 1978

CONTENTS

I
PRECURSORS

II
SPANISH

This is the earliest depiction of contact with Europeans in British Columbia, drawn by John Webber in 1778. The Mowachaht tried to direct Captain James Cook towards Yuquot by shouting "go around, go around," but Cook misinterpreted their words and gestures, giving rise to the word Nootka.

FOREWORD

"I pressed on, taking fresh trouble for granted."
—CAPTAIN BODEGA Y QUADRA

The first European to reside in British Columbia was the Irish soldier John MacKay who voluntarily wintered at Tahsis in 1786—seventeen years prior to the capture of John Jewitt, the American blacksmith who survived the massacre of the crew of the *Boston* to become known as the "white slave of the Nootka."

The first European woman to visit B.C. was eighteen-year-old newlywed Frances Barkley who circumnavigated the globe with her husband, making a lasting impression at Nootka Sound with her long red hair in 1787.

MacKay and Barkley were two of approximately 50 people who recorded their experiences as some of the first "invaders" to the Pacific Northwest prior to 1800. These commercially-minded or imperialistic Europeans and Americans were not invaders in the military sense, but their visits were invasive in terms of introducing radically new technologies, customs, foodstuffs, diseases and religion.

The surveyor Vancouver. The scientists Moziño and Menzies. The gentlemanly Bodega y Quadra. The persecuted scholar Malaspina. La Pérouse, the first Frenchman in B.C. Their adventures all generated publications that now collectively represent the literary beginnings of British Columbia.

The British Admiralty instructed 18th-century sea captains to confiscate all personal journals at the end of exploratory voyages. Sailors were likewise prohibited from divulging where they had gone until permission was given to do so. Four of Captain

James Cook's crew nonetheless beat England's most celebrated mariner to the literary punch.

John Rickman published his travelogue anonymously in 1781; Heinrich Zimmerman published in German in 1781; William Ellis published in 1782; and the remarkable John Ledyard—the Marco Polo of the United States—published his account of visiting Nootka Sound in 1783.

Cook's posthumous chronicle appeared to much acclaim in 1784. It confirmed the murdered sea captain's reputation as the world's foremost navigator and suggested that Britannia ruled the North Pacific waves. In fact, Spaniards had reached British Columbia ahead of Cook—in 1774—when Majorcan sea captain Juan Pérez opened the world's last unmapped temperate zone to exploration and European settlement.

Pérez contacted the Haida at the north end of the Queen Charlotte Islands on July 18, 1774, and his pilot produced the first crude map of the B.C. coastline to be drawn from observation.

Whereas Captains Cook and Vancouver came, saw, and published, Spain and Russia didn't broadcast their voyages. Their secrecy partially accounts for the imbalance in general knowledge of the first European approaches to B.C. to this day.

Documents are still being brought forth from Spanish, Russian and Chinese archives for translation. Meanwhile the stories of how and why scurvy-ridden sailors reached the North Pacific in the 1700s make for a fascinating hodge-podge of fact, fantasy and vainglorious quests.

In the Age of Reason, philosophers, scholars and scientists sought to dispel myths and ignorance; self-interested lobbyists such as Arthur Dobbs, Alexander Dalrymple and Joseph Banks simultaneously encouraged irrational enterprises based on speculative maps. It proved to be a fatal mix.

The Strait of Anian and the Northwest Passage were just two of the "maritime philosopher's stones." After Francis Drake dubbed the California coast Nova Albion, an opportunist named Lorenzo Ferrer Moldanado reported in 1588 that he had sailed from Iceland, across the top of Canada via Davis Strait, to the land of

Quivara in the Pacific. Other expeditions searched for Gama Land (supposedly seen by the Portuguese navigator Joaõ de Gama in 1590), Company Land (supposedly seen by an unnamed Dutch captain), and the land of Jesso (also depicted on numerous maps).

Somewhere north of Nova Albion, mariners hoped to enter the Sea of the West that Juan de Fuca had supposedly sailed within for 20 days. But most sailors were rewarded only with paralyzing cold, malnutrition, disease, harsh discipline, storms or death. The rudimentary memoirs of simple seamen such as John Nicol and Ebenezer Johnson make for fascinating but sobering accounts.

One of the most obscure literary connections to B.C. arose from the visit of the French scientist François Péron. The more I uncovered the writings of such men—and Frances Barkley—the more I wished I had known about them earlier, particularly the Spanish scientist Moziño and the American adventurer Ledyard.

In school I was never taught that Juan de Fuca was a Greek named Valerianos. If I ever had a lesson about the Nootka Incident, it didn't register. Until three years ago, I knew precious little about the most fascinating 18th-century character of them all, Chief Maquinna, or the Machiavelli of the maritime fur trade, John Meares. (The modern Mowachaht of Nootka Sound contend that Meares intentionally gave their ancestors blankets infected with disease.)

First Invaders culminates with Alexander Mackenzie's overland trek to the Pacific Ocean in 1793. It was a feat of stamina that marks the beginning of the mainland fur trade and the close of the first chapter of British Columbia's literary origins.

By "literary origins" I mean words on paper. Petroglyphs and oral storytelling have resulted in many wonderful books to date—from the anthropological probings of Franz Boas to the sophisticated analysis of Robert Bringhurst—but *First Invaders* is the first cumulative accounting of those who described Canada's West Coast in published writing resulting from visits made prior to 1800.

Letters from the late 1700s are unrepresented, as are 17th-century illustrators such as George Davidson, John Sykes, Pierre Blondela, Gaspard Duché de Vancy and Sigismund Bacstrom. With few exceptions, I've limited *First Invaders* to materials that are available in a book format. Excluded materials therefore include James Hanna's Journal of 1785; Ebenezer Dorr's Log and Journal of the *Hope*, 1790–1791; the fragmentary Log of the *Margaret*, 1792–1793; Bernard Magee's Log of the *Jefferson*, 1791–1795; Thomas Manby's *Remarks on Vancouver's Voyage* and his Log of the *Chatham*; and J. Aisley Brown's Log of the *Discovery*.

———

This book constitutes the first volume of a literary history of British Columbia. People from all over the world come to visit Friendly Cove at Nootka Sound where Captain Cook came ashore in 1778. I hope this compilation makes Canadians curious, too.

I'm most grateful for the critical input of Robin Inglis, director of the North Vancouver Archives, and Hispanic Studies professor Derek Carr; the editorial contribution of Edward Von der Porten; the spadework of many preceding authors—such as Derek Pethick, Herbert K. Beals, Derek Hayes and Jim McDowell, to name only a few—and contributors to the invaluable *British Columbia Historical News*.

My thanks go to my friend and colleague David Lester (design), my sons Jeremy (maps) and Martin (computers), agent Don Sedgwick and publisher Ronald Hatch, who made this collaborative process into a pleasure. Financial support was received from the B.C. Arts Board.

I wish to also acknowledge Grant and Lorraine Howatt of Nootka Air in Gold River who took me to Friendly Cove in rough weather, and Ray and Terry Williams, the Mowachaht protectors of Yuquot, for their hospitality and trust. —A.T.

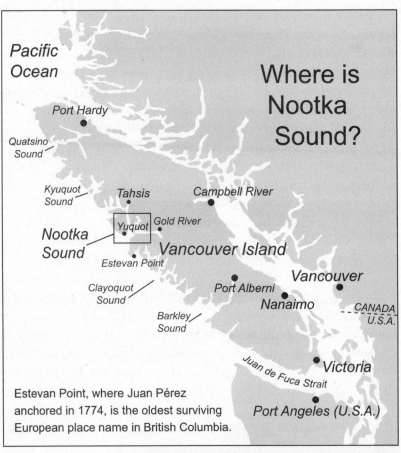

Pacific
Ocean

Where is Nootka Sound?

Port Hardy

Quatsino
Sound

Kyuquot
Sound

Tahsis

Campbell River

Nootka
Sound

Yuquot

Gold River

Vancouver Island

Estevan Point

Vancouver

Clayoquot
Sound

Port Alberni

Nanaimo

CANADA
U.S.A.

Barkley
Sound

Juan de Fuca Strait

Victoria

Estevan Point, where Juan Pérez
anchored in 1774, is the oldest surviving
European place name in British Columbia.

Port Angeles (U.S.A.)

*According to
archaeologist R.L.
Carlson, Yuquot has
the longest continuity
of Nuu-chah-nulth
habitation—
4,200 years.*

Yuquot (Friendly Cove), 1920.

Yuquot (Friendly Cove), 2004.

Jonathan Swift portrayed the West Coast of North America as a land of giants.

I
PRECURSORS

Jonathan Swift
Hui Shen
Juan de Fuca
Francis Drake
Richard Hakluyt
Samuel Purchas
Vitus Bering
Sven Waxell
Georg Wilhelm Steller
Gerhard Müller
Aleksei Chirikov
Arthur Dobbs
Denis Diderot

JONATHAN SWIFT

The first literary reference to British Columbia in English literature occurs in the second book of *Gulliver's Travels*, a fictional work by satirist Jonathan Swift, in which Gulliver sails up the northwest coast of America in 1703 to a land of giants called Brobdingnag.

This land of giants was located north of New Albion in an area roughly approximate to the locale of British Columbia. Gulliver's ship is caught in a storm "so that the oldest sailor on board could not tell in what part of the World we were."

Swift blended some known geography into his creation by incorporating the findings of world traveller William Dampier, referred to by Gulliver in the text as "my cousin, Dampier."

The term New Albion was derived from the secret voyage of Sir Francis Drake in 1579 when he was searching for a Northwest Passage back to England. In those days the dastardly Drake was the scourge of the Spanish, having plundered tons of silver and gold, so Queen Elizabeth had to be circumspect about backing the first Englishman to circumnavigate the world.

Only three copies of Drake's original "Queen's Map" were made. All copies have been destroyed or lost. Drake's charts were kept secret but his term New Albion did begin to appear on some maps that attempted to depict the western coast of North America. The first public map to record the presence of Drake on the northwest coast of America was published in a book by Richard Hakluyt in 1582.

When Swift required a setting for a mythical faraway land of giants more than a century later, New Albion was appropriated. The myth of British Columbia as a land of giants, home to the elusive Sasquatch, also has some literary roots in the journals of

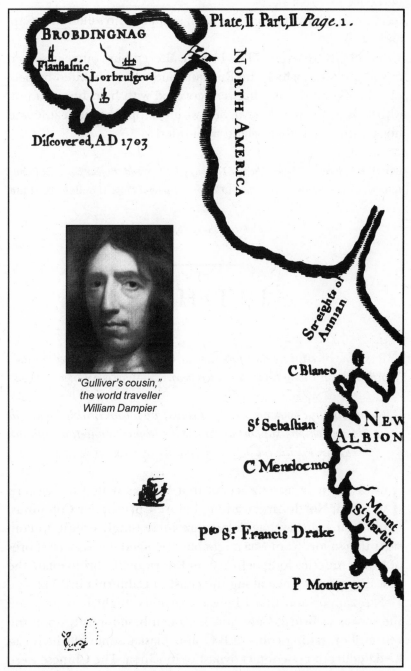

Plate, II Part, II *Page*. 1.

BROBDINGNAG

Flanflasnic

Lorbrulgrud

NORTH AMERICA

Discovered, AD 1703

Streights of Annian

C Blanco

St Sebastian

NEW ALBION

C Mendocino

Mount St Martin

Pto St Francis Drake

P Monterey

"Gulliver's cousin,"
the world traveller
William Dampier

Map in Gulliver's Travels *depicts Brobdingnag, New Albion and Francis Drake Port.*

John Ledyard, the young American seaman who sailed with Captain Cook.

John Ledyard wrote: "The 15th we altered our course in search of some islands, which the Russians said were inhabited by people of a gigantic size, who were covered with hair; but who notwithstanding were very civil, and would supply us with cattle and hogs, with which their island abounded."

BOOKS: *Travels Into Several Remote Nations Of The World. In four parts. By Lemuel Gulliver, First a Surgeon, and then a Captain of several Ships* (London: B. Motte, 1726).

—◦◦◦—

HUI SHEN

"It is a near certainty that Japanese or Chinese people arrived on the northwest coast long before any European." —HISTORIAN DEREK HAYES

"The numismatic evidence [study of coins] from both British Columbia and Alaska does not support an 'ancient Chinese' connection with the eastern Pacific coast." —ARCHAEOLOGIST GRANT KEDDIE

Just as we increasingly accept that Vikings visited the eastern shores of North America long before Christopher Columbus, historians and archaeologists are increasingly willing to consider that sailors from Asia might have reached the western shores of North America long before Juan Rodríquez Cabrillo made the first European voyage along the coast of California in 1542.

The supposition that Chinese mariners might have reached the shores of British Columbia has been based mostly upon the retrieval of trading coins in B.C. and Alaska, some of which can be dated from pre-contact dynasties in China. The Chinese were using the magnetic needle and navigating by the stars prior to the birth of Christianity. It is conceivable Asian mariners could have reached North America from China using the currents of the Pacific Ocean. Archaeologists and anthropologists in California have claimed that manganese-encrusted stone anchors discovered near Palos Verdes and off Point Mendocino in California during the 1970s are ancient Chinese artifacts but these findings have been contradicted by other scientists who claim such stone anchors and line weights were left by Chinese American fishermen in the 19th century.

Spaniards in the Gulf of California reported seeing large Chinese junks at anchor in 1544. In a controversial book entitled *1421: The Year China Discovered The World*, a retired British submarine commander named Gavin Menzies has claimed a Chinese mariner named Zheng He visited the West Coast of America about one lifetime prior to Columbus. Zheng He (1371–1435 A.D.) was a eunuch whose ships ventured to Arabia and East Africa. Such expeditions were made with flotillas of more than 300 ships under the direction of Emperor Zhu Di during the Ming Dynasty.

The cover of Gavin Menzies' book 1421: The Year China Discovered The World.

Louise Levathes' study *When China Ruled The Seas: The Treasure Fleet of the Dragon Throne, 1405–1433* (Oxford University Press, 1996) is one of several books that has documented the far-reaching accomplishments of Chinese mariners such as Zheng He (Cheng Ho), Zhou Man and Hong Bao during the early 15th century. Menzies has added a mish-mash of conjectures to Levathes' research to suggest the Chinese also reached America, Antarctica and even Europe. A media feeding frenzy ensued when Menzies' book appeared, but his research has been ridiculed as inconclusive and fanciful by academic experts.

Even more elusive are the earlier maritime wanderings of the monk Hui Shen, sometimes spelled Hoei-Shin. In *The Jade Coast* (2003), biologist Robert Butler repeats the common assertion that Hui Shen visited "a distant land to the east that they called Fusang quo" in the fifth century. This land of Fusang, Fu-Sang or Fou Sang was often included on European maps during the 18th century in areas that have roughly approximated the location of Vancouver Island.

American historian Charles Chapman refers to Hui Shen in his chapter "The Chinese Along the Pacific Coast in Ancient Times" within *A History of California: The Spanish Period.* Chris Lorenc in the *Double Cone Quarterly* repeats the supposition that Hui Shen returned to the Chinese court in 499 A.D. having named the distant land to the east after a type of plant resembling the prickly pear, cactus apple or yucca. "You can follow Hui-Shen's descriptions and distances from the Ainu in Japan," he writes, "to Kamkatcha to Fu-Sang, which measures out to California although the culture resembles people further south since the people of Fu-Sang had a form of writing and parchment made from the fu-sang plant."

Most investigators of the Hui Shen story suggest the fusang plant was the Mexican maguey plant [*Agave americana*] which served many functions for the pre-Columbian peoples of Mexico. Hui Shen reported inhabitants of Fusang were making writing paper from the plant. According to Hui Shen's narrative, houses in Fusang were constructed from wooden beams and mats were made of reeds. Other scholars have speculated as to whether Hui Shen reached Central America or went only as far as Korea.

Hui Shen's narrative about travels to an exotic land called Fusang is contained within the Chinese classic *Liang Shu* (*The History of the Liang Dynasty*). This work was first translated into English, with commentary, by the American scholar Charles G. Leland in his book *Fu-Sang, Or the Discovery of the World by Chinese Buddhist Priests in the Fifth Century* (New York: J.W. Bouton, 1875). Leland was no common sensationalist. Born in 1824, he studied at universities in Heidelberg and Munich, attended lectures at the Sorbonne, returned to Philadelphia in 1848, studied law, and

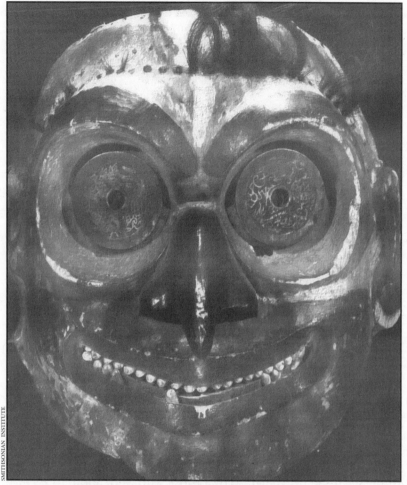

SMITHSONIAN INSTITUTE

Chilkat Tlingit mask uses Chinese temple coins for eyes.

was admitted to the bar in 1851, but made his living mainly as a writer and magazine publisher in Philadelphia and New York. Leland wrote numerous books based on his research into ancient and modern literature, translating Heinrich Heine, producing esoteric works of poetry such as *The Music Lesson of Confucius and Other Poems,* and examining subjects that included Gypsy songs, Egypt, Abraham Lincoln and Algonquin legends. Leland's investigation of Hui Shen was an expanded translation of an 1841 work by a German scholar named Carl Frederick Neumann. He, in turn, was influenced by the 1761 work of French sinologist Joseph de Guignes in the French scholarly journal *Memoires of the Academie de Belles Lettres*. The original European version of the Fusang story was entitled *Recherches sur les navigations des Chinois du côté l'Amerique.*

The Leland/Neumann translation is brief enough to provide in full. "During the reign of the dynasty Tsi, in the first year of the year-naming, 'Everlasting Origin' (A.D. 499) came a Buddhist priest from this kingdom, who bore the cloister-name of Hoei-schin, i.e., Universal Compassion, to the present district of Hukuang, and those surrounding it, who narrated that Fusang is about twenty thousand Chinese miles in an easterly direction from Tahan, and east of the Middle Kingdom. Many Fusang trees grow there, whose leaves resemble the *Dryanda cordifolia*; the sprouts, on the contrary, resemble those of the bamboo-tree, and are eaten by the inhabitants of the land. The fruit is like a pear in form, but is red. From the bark they prepare a sort of linen which they use for clothing, and also a sort of ornamented stuff [or fine silk]. The houses are built of wooden beams, fortified and walled places are there unknown.

"They have written characters in this land, and prepare paper from the bark of the Fusang. The people have no weapons, and make no wars; but in the arrangements for the kingdom they have a northern and a southern prison. Trifling offenders were lodged in the southern prison, but those confined for greater offences in the northern; so that those who were about to receive grace could be placed in the southern prison, and those who were not, in the northern. Those men and women who were imprisoned for life were allowed to marry. The boys resulting from these marriages were, at the age of eight years, sold as slaves; the girls not until their ninth year. If a man of any note was found guilty of crimes, an assembly was held; it must be in an excavated place. There they strewed ashes over him, and bade him fare-well. If the offender was one of a lower class, he alone was pun-ished; but when of rank, the degradation was extended to his children and grandchildren. With those of the highest rank it attained to the seventh generation.

"The name of the king is pronounced Ichi. The nobles of the first-class are termed Tuilu; of the second, Little Tuilu; and of the third, Na-to-scha. When the prince goes forth, he is accompanied by horns and trumpets. The colour of his clothes changes with the different years. In the two first of the ten-year cycles they are blue; in the two next, red; in the two following, yellow; in the two next, red; and in the last two, black.

"The horns of the oxen are so large that they hold ten bushels. They use them to contain all manner of things. Horses, oxen, and stags are harnessed to their wagons. Stags are used here as cattle are used in the Middle Kingdom, and from the milk of the hind they make butter. The red pears of the Fusang-tree keep good throughout the year. Moreover, they have apples and reeds. From the latter they prepare mats. No iron is found in this land; but copper, gold, and silver are not prized, and do not serve as a medium of exchange in the market.

"Marriage is determined upon in the following manner:—The suitor builds himself a hut before the door of the house where the one longed for dwells, and waters and cleans the ground every morning and evening. When a year has passed by, if the maiden is not inclined to marry him, he departs; should she be willing, it is completed. When the parents die, they fast seven days. For the death of the paternal or maternal grandfather they lament five days; at the death of elder or younger sisters or brothers, uncles or aunts, three days. They then sit from morning to evening before an image of the ghost, absorbed in prayer, but wear no mourning-clothes. When the king dies, the son who succeeds him does not busy himself for three years with State affairs.

"In earlier times these people lived not according to the laws of Buddha. But it happened that in the second year-naming 'Great Light,' of Song (A.D. 458), five beggar-monks from the kingdom of Kipin went to this land, extended over it the religion of Buddha, and with it his holy writings and images. They instructed the people in the principles of monastic life, and so changed their manners."

If Hui Shen followed the Japanese Current from the Orient to Mexico, he could have visited British Columbia en route—and his narrative might have contained the first literary reference to B.C.

The original story of Hui Shen has had a convoluted publishing history, undergoing various transmutations. It is assumed he departed from China during the Sung Dynasty based in Nanking (420–479 A.D.) but he returned during the short-lived Ch'i Dynasty (479–502 A.D.). Records for the Ch'i Dynasty were lost but his adventures were mentioned in documents pertaining to the Liang Dynasty (502–557 A.D.). These records also disappeared but extracts subsequently were published in *The History of the Liang Dynasty*, or the *Liang Shu*, completed around 629 A.D. by a team of official Chinese historians that included Yao Silian (557–637 A.D.). The *Liang Shu* recalls a monk named Hui Shen sailed across the great eastern sea between 458 A.D. and 499 A.D. to reach the land of Fusang. Almost seven centuries later, the adventures of Hui Shen were extracted from the Liang Shu for Ma Tuanlin's historical encyclopedia called *Wen-hsien t'ung-K'ao* in 1317 A.D. That version of Hui Shen's story was, in turn, translated by de Guignes in 1761 A.D., to be followed by subsequent translations of de Guignes' version into English by Leland (1875), Edward Vining (1885) and Henriette Mertz (1972).

"A modern and critical translation of the original documents is needed," wrote Grant Keddie of the Royal British Columbia Museum in 1989, "before there can be an attempt to resolve the dispute as to the locations referred to in the stories."

Amen to that.

BOOKS: *Liang Shu (The History of the Liang Dynasty)*, 629 A.D., column 54, Dong Yi Lie Zhuan, edited by Si'lian Yao, Tang Dynasty. **British:** *Fusang, Or the Discovery of the World by Chinese Buddhist Priests in the Fifth Century* (1875; Curzon Press Ltd. 1973). **American:** *Fusang or the Discovery of America by Chinese Buddhist Priests in the Fifth Century* by Charles G. Leland (New York: Bouton, 1875, 8 vol; Harper & Row, 1973); *An Inglorious Columbus: Or Evidence that Hwui Shan and a Party of Buddhist Monks from Afghanistan discovered America in the Fifth Century*

A.D. by Edward Vinning (New York, Appleton-Century-Crofts, 1885); *Fusang: Or the Discovery of America by Chinese Buddhist Priests in the Fifth Century* by Charles G. Leland (Sun Publishing, 1981); *Pale Ink: Two Ancient Records of Chinese Exploration in America* by Henriette Mertz (Chicago: The Swallow Press, 1972); *1421: The Year China Discovered the World* by Gavin Menzies (Morrow, 2003).

JUAN DE FUCA

Juan de Fuca was a Greek named Apostolos Valerianos who, in the service of Spain, might have been the first European to reach British Columbia.

Some evidence that Juan de Fuca was the first European to discover the strait between Vancouver Island and Washington State that bears his name is provided in a remarkable compilation of travel literature called *Hakluytus Posthumus* or *Purchas His Pilgrimes Contayning a History of the World in Sea Voyages and Lande Travells by Englishmen and others* in 1625. Purchas based his evidence about Juan de Fuca on letters written by an Englishman named John Lok who met Juan de Fuca in Venice, Italy, in 1596. Impressed by Juan de Fuca's claims to have sailed up the west coast of North America, Lok wrote to the Lord Treasurer, to Sir Walter Raleigh and to Master Richard Hakluyt asking them to send £100 to bring de Fuca to England. Juan de Fuca departed for Cephalonia before Lok could succeed in having money sent. Samuel Purchas later wrote, "In the year 1592 the Viceroy of Mexico sent a pilot named Juan de Fuca on a voyage of discovery to the northwest. De Fuca followed the coast until he came to the latitude of 47º and there finding that a broad inlet trended to the eastward between the latitudes of 47º and 48º, he sailed up it for more than twenty days." If Juan de Fuca indeed sailed up the Strait of Juan de Fuca for 20 days, obviously he ventured as far as present-day British Columbia.

According to the Consulate of Greece in Vancouver, Valerianos/Juan de Fuca was born on the island of Cephalonia in the Ionian Sea. He went to Spain and worked as a mariner and a pilot for 40 years. In November 1587 on a return voyage from the Philippines and China on the *Santa Anna*, Valerianos was overtaken by the English Captain Candish who stole his cargo valued at some 60,000 ducats. Several years later, Valerianos was sent by the Viceroy of Mexico to serve as the pilot for an expedition of three small ships and 200 soldiers to find the Strait of Anian, the long hoped-for Northwest Passage back to Europe as envisioned by Sir Francis Drake. This expedition failed due to mutiny and the alleged misconduct of the captain in charge. The ships returned from California to Mexico. Undeterred, the Viceroy of Mexico sent Valerianos (Juan de Fuca) once more northward with a small caravela and a pinnace, hoping they could discover a route to the North Sea. On this voyage Juan de Fuca allegedly entered the strait that bears his name and saw people clothed in animal skins. He allegedly returned to Acapulco in 1592 where he was honoured for his efforts. After waiting two years for his promised rewards that were never forthcoming, he went to Spain to collect his payment from the Spanish king. Although Juan de Fuca was well-treated at court, he was unable to gain any rewards beyond flattery. Disgusted, he left Spain for Cephalonia, stopping in Venice in 1596.

In conversation with Michael Lok, an English Consul, the Greek/Spanish mariner offered his services to the Queen of England if England wanted to discover the Northwest Passage. He agreed to serve as a pilot if Queen Elizabeth provided a ship of 40 tons. He also hoped the English would provide compensation for goods that were stolen from him by Captain Candish. Lok wrote to England, but the matter could not be resolved quickly. Juan de Fuca returned to his homeland. Lok wrote to Juan de Fuca in 1602 but no reply was received. The English presumed Juan de Fuca, already an old man when he met John Lok, must have died.

In 1847, American historian Robert Greenhow published a

One of the first views of Juan de Fuca Strait was drawn by T. Stothard in 1788 for John Meares' 1790 book. It depicts the Makha Indians meeting the longboat of the Feliz near the entrance to Juan de Fuca Strait. Vancouver Island is on the left and Cape Flattery is on the right. In the right background is Tatoosh Island and majestic Mount Olympus, renamed by Meares after Juan Pérez had named it Cerra de Santa Rosalía in 1774.

history of Oregon and California in which he supplied a summary of Juan de Fuca's life based upon the English and Spanish translations of the correspondence between de Fuca and Lok. In 1854, another American historian named Alexander S. Taylor took up the narrative by asking the American Consul in the Ionian Islands, A.S. York, to gather any and all material concerning Juan de Fuca and his family.

York provided information gleaned from *The Lives of Glorious Men of Cephalonia* written and published in Venice in October 1843 by Rev. Anthimos Mazarakis, a Cephalonian. The book had been translated into Italian by Tomazeo. Taylor published two articles in the September and October 1859 issues of *Hutchings' California Magazine* that recounted what he had gleaned about Juan de Fuca's life.

According to Taylor's research, the ancestors of John Phokas (Fucas) fled Constantinople in 1453 and found refuge in the Ionian Islands. Andronikos Phokas remained as the head of the Phokas family. His brother named Emmanuel Phokas was born in Constantinople in 1435 and departed in 1470 for Cephalonia. He settled in a valley in southwestern Cephalonia at Elios. In that valley lies the village of Valeriano. Juan de Fuca was one of four sons born to Emmanuel Phokas, also known as Phokas Valerianos to distinguish him from the Phokas family in Argostoli.

According to the Greek Consulate of Vancouver, "The extension of the Spanish dominion in the neighboring shores of Italy and the commercial relations which sprang up as a result with the Ionian Islands, gave the opportunity to the seafaring men of the Ionian Islands to serve in Spanish ships as crews or officers. Fucas, driven by such an ambition, went to Spain where he embarked on Spanish ships sailing over the oceans. In a very short time he learned the art of pilotage so well that he attracted the attention of the King of Spain who appointed him Pilot of his navy in the West Indies, a position which he kept for over forty years."

As conveyed by Lok and recorded by Purchas, Juan de Fuca claimed the entranceway to the great inlet between 47º and 48º was marked by "an exceedingly high pinnacle or spired rock, like a pillar, thereupon." Coastal historian Captain John T. Walbran corroborated this report in *British Columbia Coast Names*. He wrote, "This is substantially correct; the island is Tatooche, and the spired rock, now known as De Fuca's pillar, 150 feet high, stands in solitary grandeur, a little off shore, about two miles southwards of Tatooche Island." The first English mariner to recognize Juan de Fuca's strait was Captain Charles Barkley on the *Imperial Eagle* in 1787. He consequently named Juan de Fuca Strait because it lay above the 47th parallel, where Lok's report of Juan de Fuca's exploration had designated it to be. Having had access to Frances Barkley's diary of her husband's 1787 voyage, Captain Walbran recorded the perceptions of that voyage. "The entrance appeared to be about four leagues in width, and remained about that width as far as the eye can see. Capt. Barkley at once recognized it as the long lost strait of Juan de Fuca, which Captain Cook had so emphatically stated did not exist." Captain Barkley concluded Juan de Fuca must have been the first foreign mariner to round the point now called Cape Flattery, but Barkley himself did not venture into the opening.

BOOKS: Anthimos Mazarakis, *The Lives of Glorious Men of Cephalonia* (Venice, 1843).

FRANCIS DRAKE

The deadly privateer Sir Francis Drake gave the western U.S. its first European-based name—Nova Albion, essentially New England—but historians agree to disagree about whether or not Drake might have sailed above the 49th parallel prior to Juan de Fuca or any other European. Details of Drake's heroic 1577–1580 global voyage to "the very end of the world from us" were mainly recorded by the Cambridge-educated cleric Francis Fletcher who kept a journal on board the *Golden Hind*. "Whether Drake reached the coast as far north as the Strait of Juan de Fuca," according to Derek Hayes, author of *Historical Atlas of British Columbia and the Pacific Northwest*, "is likely to remain a puzzle."

The site of Drake's Harbour, called Portus Nova Albion, where Drake took possession of the coast in the name of the Queen of England, is sometimes ascribed to Whale Cove on the Oregon coast or various bays in California. In 2003, Samuel Bawlf transformed and expanded his self-published Ph.D. thesis on Sir Francis Drake for a controversial biography that strongly suggests Drake was indeed the first European to reach British Columbia in 1579, but there is no conclusive evidence. Despite the packaging of Bawlf's *The Secret Voyage of Sir Francis Drake* as a revelation, he is not the first historian to propose the Drake-Came-First theory. In 1927, the prolific social reformer A.M. Stephen of Vancouver published his first novel, *The Kingdom of the Sun*, about a gentleman adventurer named Richard Anson who sailed aboard

Drake's *Golden Hind*, only to be cast away among the Haida and fall in love with a Haida princess.

The eldest of twelve brothers, Francis Drake was born in Tavistock, Devon, around 1542. The Drake family had lost property when King Henry VIII founded the Church of England in defiance of Rome. Drake was sent to live with his seafaring kin, the Hawkins family. Leaving Plymouth in 1562, Drake likely accompanied John Hawkins down the Guinea coast to acquire slaves from present-day Sierra Leone. As a Caribbean slave trader in 1568, Drake was at the helm of *Judith*, two days after entering the principal Mexican port of San Juan d' Ulúa, when Hawkins' outmanned flotilla was attacked by the Spanish with terrifying results. Drake fled the harbor, leaving hundreds of desperate English sailors stranded. "The *Judith* forsooke us in our great myserie," said one of Hawkins' men. The romantic ethic of "one for all and all for one" was not for Drake. He was a charming, self-serving man, loathed by many in London and around the world.

The clash with Spain gained Drake his lifelong right to function as a privateer, in essence, a legalized pirate. Drake quickly became famous for his looting of Spanish galleons. He made profitable voyages in 1570 and 1571, trading slaves in the West Indies, then commanded two ships in 1572 to specifically attack the Spanish. Spanish mothers took to frightening their children into good behavior with tales of "El Draque," the Dragon. Drake was known as a harsh taskmaster. When one of his brothers died at sea, he proceeded to have the body dissected to find the cause of his death. Impressed by his daring, Queen Elizabeth sent him on a secret mission to plunder Spanish settlements on the Pacific Coast of the New World in 1577.

Drake departed on December 13, 1577, and quickly reached Morocco, losing a boy overboard en route from the supply ship *Swan*, the first of his many casualties. Drake got lucky in early February when he commandeered a Portuguese ship off the Cape Verde Islands, kidnapping its veteran captain Nuño da Silva who had sailed to Brazil many times since his boyhood. In the process, Drake acquired charts for his Atlantic voyage and soundings for the South American coast as far south as Rio de la Plata. He would employ a similar tactic, with equal success, when he reached the Pacific. Drake crossed the equator on February 17, 1578. In South America they met Indians who never cut their hair, knitting it with ostrich feathers to form a quiver for their arrows. Accusing the troublesome investor Thomas Doughty of treachery, Drake had his adversary executed by ax on July 2, 1578. For food, the crew slaughtered sea lions and penguins. They found the bones of a Spanish mutineer named Gaspar Quesada killed by Magellan in 1522. With his crew afflicted by scurvy and cold temperatures, Drake discovered that a stew of mussels and seaweed could be restorative.

Sir Francis Drake

Upon entering the perilous Strait of Magellan, Drake changed the name of his heavily armed flagship from the *Pelican* to the *Golden Hind.* The land south of the strait was called Tierra del Fuego (land of fires) because Indians had lit fires as Magellan had sailed past. On one day in August, Drake's remaining men slaughtered 3,000 penguins, enough food to last 40 days. After only 16 days battling the currents and the foul weather, they reached the Pacific on September 6, 1578. This was new territory for England. Of the five ships sent, two had already been abandoned before reaching the southern tip of the South American continent. Of the remaining three ships, one was destroyed by violent storms and another sailed back to England. Drake was blown far south but travelled back up the coast. Beset by storms, his crew eventually set sail for the Kingdom of Peru with 80 men and boys, sailing 1,200 miles without stopping. On the island of Mocha, at 38° south, initially friendly Indians attacked their landing party, killing several men with a flurry of arrows. Fletcher recorded in his journal that no one escaped being hit. "Drake was hit twice, one penetrating his face under his right eye and another creasing his scalp." One crewman was punctured by 21 arrows.

The Spanish were aghast that Drake had become the first English sea captain to replicate Magellan's path. Their build-up of ports from modern-day California to Chile had been accomplished primarily via overland routes through Panama. Their relatively undefended Pacific ports and shipping made for easy pickings. Drake went to work sacking towns and attacking ships to acquire maps and provisions. During his piratical triumphs, Drake took aboard a black slave as his concubine. Maria, as she was named, was "gotten with child between the captain and his men pirates" and she was to be marooned on an Indonesian island to have the child, along with two black slaves for company.

Drake headed north; a few say as far as today's U.S./Canada border. He named this uncharted coastal realm New Albion. According to memoirs of the voyage, this name was given "for two causes: the one in respect of the white bancks and cliffes, which lie toward the sea: the other that it might haue some affinity, euen in name also, with our owne country, which was sometimes so called."

Unable to find a passage home via the imagined Strait of Anian, Drake headed westward across the Pacific, through the islands of Indonesia and finally around the Cape of Good Hope at the bottom of Africa. Drake made it back to England by September of 1580, bearing an enormous cache of spices and Spanish booty. Queen Elizabeth knighted Drake aboard the *Golden Hind* for his efforts. Drake was the first sea captain to fully circumnavigate the world. Magellan had died en route, and his crew had completed the voyage.

Naval charts were precious and kept secret during the Elizabethan era. This was especially so with Drake's round-the-world trip. His charts and rough maps could not be publicized for fear of Spanish competition and reprisals. *The World Encompassed by Sir Francis Drake* was eventually published by Drake's nephew, also named Francis Drake, in 1628. Published in 2003, R. Samuel

Bawlf's *Sir Francis Drake and his Secret Voyage 1577–1580* outlines why Drake's voyage up the "backside of Canada" has long remained mysterious and controversial.

Bawlf writes, "In time, Drake began giving hand-drawn maps depicting his route around the world to important friends. In an early rendition, drawn with pen and ink on the world map of Abraham Ortelius, his route extended northward along the coast of North America to latitude 57º—the latitude of Southern Alaska—before returning south and homeward via the East Indies. Then, with the help of a young Flemish artist named Jodocus Hondius, Drake produced several more maps. On these maps his track northward terminated at a lower latitude, where an inscription read 'turned back on account of the ice,' and then returned southward to a place called Nova Albion."

R. Samuel Bawlf's favourable portrait of Drake has proved to be a source of consternation for some serious Drake scholars because it allegedly crafts some conjectures into implied truths. (See page 224.)

Testimony that Drake had ventured up the Pacific Coast, past California, was gained by the Spanish by March 24, 1584, when John Drake, Drake's brother, was formally brought before the Inquisition during his captivity in Argentina. John Drake was interrogated again in Lima, Peru on January 8, 9 and 10, 1587. The gist of John Drake's confessions about his role in Francis Drake's secret voyage, reliable or not, was published by Antonio de Herrera, the Historian General of New Spain, in 1606. John Drake's testimony is stored in the Spanish archives of Seville.

Emerging Protestant attitudes stressed individual achievement—in essence, if you could make money, this meant God favoured you. Drake won God's favour as a privateer. He was the harbinger of a new age, essentially a self-made man. The once lowly seaman became mayor of Plymouth in 1581 and a Member of Parliament in 1584. In 1585 Drake led a large fleet to the Caribbean to terrorize the ports of Spanish America. Sir Francis Drake's plundering was so successful in the Caribbean that he ruined Spanish credit, nearly breaking the Bank of Venice to which Spain was heavily indebted.

Drake gained permanent heroic status in the annals of English history by playing a major role in the defeat of the once all-powerful Spanish Armada in 1588. But the Spanish navy wasn't completely destroyed. Four Spanish ships made a daring raid on Penzance in Cornwall, destroying the village of Mousehole, in July of 1595. Drake continued stalking the Spanish. He suggested a raid on Panama and the Queen agreed. During this fruitless mission, he contracted dysentery ("the bloody flux") at Panama and died on January 29, 1596. Officially, Francis Drake "dyed without Issue" and was buried at sea.

BOOKS: Francis Fletcher, *The World Encompassed by Sir Francis Drake* (London: Nicholas Bourne, 1628); *The World Encompassed by Sir Francis Drake*, ed. W. S. W. Vaux (London: Hakluyt Society, 1856).

━━━━◦◦◦◦◦━━━━

RICHARD HAKLUYT

Clergyman Richard Hakluyt provided the first published account of Sir Francis Drake's circumnavigation of the globe, summarizing Drake's explorations on the California coast. He did not provide any confirmation that Drake sailed as far north as British Columbia. In 1582 he published the first map to indicate Drake's presence on the Northwest Pacific Coast, a distorted misrepresentation first given to Henry VIII by Giovanni da Verrazano, and later provided to Hakluyt by Michael Lok. This map was immediately followed by "The French Drake Map" of Nicola van Sype, circa 1583, and the 1589 map of Joducus Hondius that depicts Portus Nova Albionis, or Drake's Harbour.

Hakluyt was a clergyman who lectured on geography at the University of Oxford. He befriended sea captains and merchants, gathering intelligence on the Pacific fur trade and other foreign

118.	The Engliſh Voyages, Nauigations,						M. John Davis. 3

Moneth Iuly.	Dayes	Houres	Courſe	Leagues	Elevation of the pole. Deg	Min	The winde	THE DISCOVRSE.
	31	24	☉.by ☉	27	62		N.W.	This 31 at noone, comming close by a tremeteo or great cape, we fell into a mightie rase, where an illand of ice was carried by the force of the current as fast as our barke could saile with him winde, all sailes bearing. This cape was the most Southerly limit of the gulfe which we passed ouer: the 30 day of this moneth, so was it the North promontory or first beginning of another very great inlet, whose South limit at this present wee saw not. Which inlet or gulfe this afternoone, and in the night, we passed ouer: where to our great admiration we saw the sea falling downe into the gulfe with a mighty ouerfall, and roring, and with diuers circular motions like whirlepooles, in such sort as forcible streames passe thorow the arches of bridges.
August								
Noone the 1	24	☉.E.by ☉.	16	61	10	W.S.W.	The true courſe, &c. This first of August we fell with the promontory of the sayd gulfe or second passage, hauing coasted by diuers courses for our saue-
Noone the 2	48	☉.☉.E.	16	60	26	Variable.	gard, a great banke of the ice driuen out of that gulfe.
Noone the 6	72	☉.E.Southerly.	22	59	35	Variable to calme.	The true courſe, &c.
7	24	☉.☉.E.	22	58	40	W.S.W.	The true courſe.&c.
8	24	☉.E.	12	58	12	W. fog.	The true courſe.&c.
9	24	☉.by W.	13	57	30	Variable & calme.	The true courſe.&c.

John Davis' logbook from The Principall Navigations compiled by Richard Hakluyt.

commercial enterprises, and he published all available information on British voyages. The third part of his major work in 1589 concerns North America and the Northwest Passage.

Hakluyt also recorded reports of a Portuguese sailor named Antonio Galvão who had visited China in 1555 and reported stories of Chinese voyages to the New World. This historical hearsay was enhanced by Galvão's observations about the similarities in appearance between New World and Chinese peoples. Hakluyt advised Elizabeth I until her death in 1603 and he became a charter member of the Northwest Passage Company in 1612. Possibly born around 1552, Hakluyt died in 1616.

Inspired by Richard Hakluyt, the non-profit Hakluyt Society was founded in 1846 and it continues to publish and promote public knowledge of records of voyages, travels and geographical discovery. It operates in care of the Map Library, British Museum. It publishes on average two volumes per year, with its membership open to anyone interested in geographical discoveries and cultural encounters.

BOOKS: *Divers Voyages touching the discovery of America* (London, 1582); *The Principall* [sic] *Navigations, Voiages, and Discoveries of the English Nation* [...] (London: George Bishop and Ralph Newberie, 1589); *The Principal Navigations, Voyages, Traffiques and Discoveries of the English Nation* (London, 1600).

SAMUEL PURCHAS

Samuel Purchas, the greatest compiler of English seafaring literature, never travelled more than 200 miles from his birthplace but he played a pivotal role in the literary history of Canada and British Columbia.

Born in Essex (exact date unknown), Purchas (pronounced Pur-kas) was ordained in 1578. He served as chaplain to the Archbishop of Canterbury and later became the rector of St. Martin's Church in London.

His first important publication was a translation of Jacques Cartier's travel memoir, *Cartier's Short and Briefe Narration* (1580), followed by *Divers Voyages*, dedicated to Sir Philip Sidney, and *Discourse on the Western Planting* (1584) for Walter Raleigh. He presented Queen Elizabeth with an analysis of Aristotle's *Politics* and he completed a translation of Laudonnière's travels to Florida in 1587.

In 1613 Purchas published his first major book, with an unwieldy title, as his initial attempt to survey the peoples and religions of the world.

Purchas then used the papers of Richard Hakluyt and East India Company records, plus many manuscripts he had gathered during his lifetime, to produce his famous omnibus about travel literature. It is known as *Hakluytus Posthumus*, or *Purchas His Pilgrims*. Although Purchas died in the year following its publication, it has remained a long-standing reference work, republished in various editions through the centuries, such as *Hakluytus Posthumus, or Purchas His Pilgrimes: Contayning a History of the World in Sea Voyages and Lande Travells by Englishmen and Others*. (Glasgow: James MacLehose and Sons, 1906).

This immense work influenced North Pacific exploration due

Title page from Samuel Purchas' book published in 1613.

to its references to a broad inlet between the latitudes of 47º and 48º, as sailed by Juan de Fuca. Was this the Strait of Anian?

Captain James Cook, sailing along the coast in 1778, scoffed at the purported existence of such any wide opening eastward.

"We saw nothing like it," Cook wrote. "Nor is there the least probability that ever such thing existed." In fact, Cook had been blown off-coast and simply missed it.

Samuel Purchas became a consultant for the East India Company in 1599 and he died in London in 1626.

BOOKS: *Purchas, his pilgrimage or relations of the world and the religions observed in all ages and places discovered, from the Creation unto this Present. In foure partes. This first containeth a Theologicall and Geographicall Historie of Asia, Africa and America, with the Ilands adjacent. Declaring the ancient Religions before the Floud, heathenish, Jewish and Saracenicall in all ages since, in these parts professed, with their severall Opinions, Idols, Oracles, Temples, Priestes, Fasts, Feasts, Sacrifices and Rites, rligious, etc. With briefe descriptions of the Countries, Nations, States, Discoueries, etc.* (William Stansley, London, 1613, 1614, 1617); *Hakluytus Posthumus, or Purchas His Pilgrims,* 4 vol. (London: Henrie Fetherstone, 1625).

VITUS BERING

"We do not know this country, nor are we supplied with provisions to keep us through the winter." —VITUS BERING

Although Russian expeditions in the 18th century reached California, and Japanese sailors reached Mexico and California even earlier, there are no recorded Russian or Japanese landfalls in British Columbia territory. Aleksei Chirikov came closest in 1741, but by far the most famous of the Russian explorers via Asia was the Danish-born Commander Vitus Jonassen Bering, whose activities had an enormous influence upon subsequent maritime explorers of the Pacific Northwest.

Vitus Bering is often wrongly credited with confirming the separation of the two continents in 1728. Bering was not the first Russian to sail into the Bering Strait. That distinction was earned by a little-known Siberian Cossack, Semen Ivanovitch Dezhnev, who sailed around the extreme northeastern tip of Siberia in 1648.

Of the seven small ships that Dezhnev led from the mouth of the Kolyma River, with 90 men aboard, only two ships returned. No ship's log or maps survive—but some historians have concluded Vitus Bering knew about Dezhnev's voyage into the Arctic, for three reasons: A Dutchman named Nicholaas Witsen had visited Moscow in 1665 and gathered enough geographical information to publish a four-sheet map of Russia in 1687 and this map incorporated both the Kolyma and Anadyr Rivers, the latter river being the furthermost point, at about 176º east, that Dezhnev had reached. Secondly, a report on Bering's maritime feats in the *St. Petersburg Gazette* in 1730 states that Bering had "learned from the local inhabitants that fifty or sixty years before a vessel arrived in Kamchatka from the Lena," likely a reference to Dezhnev. Thirdly, and most conclusively, in 1786, a scientist named Gerhard Müller, who was on the Great Northern Expedition, uncovered a written account of Dezhnev's 1648 voyage in eastern Siberia at the government offices in Yakutsk.

Müller made a map based on the information about Dezhnev's voyage. Verification of Dezhnev's accomplishment was not printed in Russian until 1742. This 1742 report was not widely circulated until the Russian Academy of Sciences re-published the information in 1758. By this time the strait that separates Asia and North America had already been named after Bering.

Born in 1681 in Horsens, Denmark, Bering served for 38 years with the Russian fleet and was encouraged secretly to explore the North Pacific by Tsar Peter the Great. The written record for his final doomed adventure was rendered for posterity mainly by his second-in-command, the Swede Sven Waxell and his German-born scientist Georg Wilhelm Steller. Along with Ferdinand Magellan and James Cook, Bering never survived his final voyage.

Bering's last expedition sailed on the *Peter* in September, 1740, from Okhotsk accompanied by the *Paul* under the command of Aleksei Chirikov. After wintering in Kamchatka, Bering and Chirikov sailed into the Pacific

Undoctored, this is the only portrait of Vitus Bering.

Ocean from Petrovskaia (Petropavlovsk) in June of 1741. The two commanders became permanently separated by fog or storms on June 20.

When Bering first sailed through the Bering Strait in 1728 aboard the *St. Gabriel*, he had been instructed by Peter the Great in 1725 "to find out where it [Asia] joins America...." But Bering had failed on that mission. Beset by fog and proceeding only as far as 67º north, he never conclusively proved that Asia and North America were separate continents. The first Russian mariner to glimpse North America, Michael Gvozdev, recorded his sighting of a "large country" (*bolshaya zemlya*) while sailing east of Siberia in 1732.

It's often assumed that Bering must have accomplished the first proven landfall on the north Pacific Coast by Europeans during his final voyage in 1741. In fact, Bering's sailing partner, Aleksei Chirikov, preceded Bering's landing by five days when his crew made landfall north of Dixon Entrance, in Alaskan territory, on July 15, 1741.

The first landfall in North America by Bering's men occurred at a place in the Aleutian chain now called Kayak Island. Bering's men first sighted Mount St. Elias on July 17, 1741. A landing party led by Fleet Master Sofron Khitrov used a longboat to go ashore several days later on July 20. Bering named this place St. Elias Island in honour of the Russian saint's day. Khitrov sketched a map in his logbook, the first Russian map exclusively to represent territory in North America. Mount St. Elias received its name later and St. Elias Island was renamed Kayak Island.

When Bering's expedition first sighted North American land on July 17, Bering was congratulated by his men but he was not cheerful. He told his scientist Georg Steller, "We think now we have accomplished everything, and may go about greatly inflated, but they do not consider where we have reached land, how far we are from home, and what may yet happen. Who knows but that perhaps trade winds may arise which may prevent us from returning? We do not know this country, nor are we supplied with provisions to keep us through the winter."

Bering's words were prophetic. Vitus Bering died on December 8, 1741 on Bering Island, east of Kamchatka. Details of Bering's ill-fated expedition are mainly recorded by Sven Waxell, G.W. Steller and the logbooks that have survived.

BOOKS: Gerhard Friedrich Müller, *Nachricten von Seareisen* (St. Petersburg: 1758) and translated by Carol Furness as *Bering's Voyages: The Reports from Russia by Gerhard Friedrich Müller* (University of Alaska Press, 1986); Peter Lauridsen, *Vitus Bering: The Discoverer of Bering Strait* (Denmark, 1885) and translated by Julius E. Olson in an American edition with an introduction by Frederick Schwatka (Chicago: S.C. Griggs, 1981); J.L. Smith, *The First Kamchatka Expedition of Vitus Bering, 1725–1730* (Anchorage, Alaska: White Stone Press, 2002); Orcutt Frost, *Bering: The Russian Discovery of America* (Yale University Press, 2003).

———◦◦◦———

SVEN WAXELL

Sven Waxell (1701-1762) was the Swedish second-in-command to Vitus Bering when his men made their North American landfall. This expedition used a wildly speculative 1731 map drawn by Joseph-Nicolas de L'Isle, revised in 1733.

Bering, at age sixty, was ill with scurvy early in the voyage and Waxell had control of the ship's day-to-day operations. Accompanied by his twelve-year-old son, Waxell produced the best-known account of the fateful expedition, although Bering's log was also kept by his assistant navigator, Kharlam Yushin.

Waxell wrote, "By now so many of our people were ill that I had, so to speak, no one to steer the ship. Our sails, too, had worn so thin that I expected them to fly off at any moment. When it came to a man's turn at the helm, he was dragged to it by two other of the invalids who were still able to walk a little, and set down at the wheel. There he had to sit and steer as well as he could, and when he could sit no more, he had to be replaced by

With Swedish writing, this map by Waxell depicts a fur seal, a sea lion and a sea cow.

another in no better case than he.... Our ship was like a piece of dead wood, with none to direct it. We had to drift hither and thither at the whim of the winds and waves. I tried to instill courage into the men, appealing to them; for there was no question of exerting authority in such a situation, where desperation already held sway."

With 12 crew members already dead, a group decision was made on November 4, 1741, to try anchoring near some land they sighted, presuming they had reached Kamchatka on the Russian mainland. In fact, this was Bering Island, located about 175 km. from Kamchatka. Their ship was unable to properly anchor due to the harsh conditions of wind and surf and was gradually torn asunder as the death toll mounted. The blue foxes on Bering Island ate the hands and feet of the dead before they could be buried. "Men were continually dying," Waxell wrote of that winter. "Our plight was so wretched that the dead had to lie for a considerable time among the living, for there was none able to drag corpses away, nor were those who lived capable of moving away from the dead. They had to remain lying all mixed up together in a ring with a little fire in the centre." During his final voyage Vitus Bering was mostly too ill to perform even the job of making journal entries. When Bering died, Waxell formally took command and presented the official record of the expedition.

BOOKS: *Journal of Captain-Commander Vitus Bering and Lieutenant Sven Waxell 1741–1742 from Petrovskaia Harbor to the East written on the boat Petr, from May 24, 1741 to September 7, 1742;* Sven Waxell, *The American Expedition* (London: William Hodge and Company, 1952); *The Russian Expedition to America,* with an introduction and notes by M. A. Michael (first published as *The American Expedition*) (New York: Collier Books, 1962).

GEORG WILHELM STELLER

Steller's jay (*Cyanocitta stelleri*) was officially adopted as the provincial bird of British Columbia in 1987. Steller's name is also attached to the Steller's sea eagle.

German-born naturalist Georg Wilhelm Steller (1709-1746) was one of the 46 men among Vitus Bering's original crew of 78. They were the first Europeans to spend a winter on the North Pacific Coast of North America. A variety of the now extinct Great Northern Manatee (*Hydrodamalis gigas*), or sea cow, is named for him. Steller's sea cows measured up to 25 feet in length and 22 feet around, sometimes weighing more than 8,800 pounds. They were hunted relentlessly for their meat and were soon extinct.

Georg Steller measures a sea cow on Bering Island.
Illustration by Leonard Stejneger, from Bering's Voyages *by F.A. Golder (1925).*

Arrogant and intelligent, Steller was critical of the competency of Bering and his subordinates aboard the *Peter.* "They mocked, ridiculed and cast to the winds whatever was said by anyone not a seaman as if with the rules for navigation all science and powers of reasoning were spontaneously acquired." Steller had to protest vociferously to Bering in order to be allowed to go ashore for ten frantic hours during which he assiduously recorded the remarkable array of new creatures. Steller's care and his provision of fresh greens and meat later enabled Sven Waxell and his son to survive the winter. Waxell subsequently oversaw the construction of a fragile ship from the wreckage of the *Peter* with which they managed to sail back to the Kamchatka mainland, returning 14 months after leaving port. Like Waxell, Steller produced an account of the voyage, later published in 1793.

Steller's journal was discovered in the Russian archives in 1917 by Frank Golder.

BOOKS: Georg Wilhelm Steller, *Reise von Kamtschatka nach Amerika mit dem Commandeur-Capitan Bering: ein Pendant zu dessen Beschreibung von Kamtschatka* (St. Petersburg: Johann Zacharias Logan, 1793); *Journal of a Voyage with Bering 1741–1742* is the original 1743 manuscript edited and with an introduction by O.W. Frost; translated by Margritt A. Engel and O.W. Frost (Stanford, California: Stanford University Press, 1988).

GERHARD MÜLLER

Having served with Vitus Bering as the head of the academic section of the Great Northern Expedition, the German scholar and scientist Gerhard Müller combined his knowledge of Bering's 1728 and 1741 voyages with his knowledge of Semen Dezhnev's 1648 voyage to produce maps in 1754 and 1758 that best represented the known geography of the North Pacific.

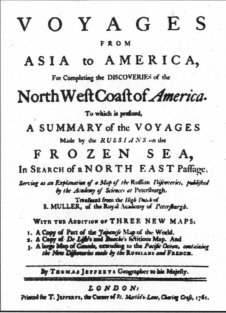

VOYAGES

FROM

ASIA to AMERICA,

For Completing the DISCOVERIES of the

North West Coast of America.

To which is prefixed,

A SUMMARY of the VOYAGES

Made by the RUSSIANS on the

FROZEN SEA,

In SEARCH of a NORTH EAST Paffage.

Serving as an Explanation of a Map of the Ruffian Difcoveries, published
by the Academy of Sciences at Peterfburgh.

Tranflated from the High Dutch of
S. MULLER, of the Royal Academy of Peterfburgh.

WITH THE ADDITION OF THREE NEW MAPS;

1. A Copy of Part of the Japanefe Map of the World.
2. A Copy of De Lifle's and Buache's fictitious Map. And
3. A large Map of Canada, extending to the Pacific Ocean, containing
the New Difcoveries made by the RUSSIANS and FRENCH.

By THOMAS JEFFERYS Geographer to his Majefty.

LONDON:

Printed for T. JEFFERYS, the Corner of St. Martin's-Lane, Charing Crofs, 1761.

Title page of Gerhard Müller's book in English,
translated by Thomas Jefferys in 1761.
Müller's influential map first appeared in
the original 1758 German edition.

Müller had come to St. Petersburg from Leipzig in 1725. He later became permanent secretary of the Russian Imperial Academy of Sciences after he had spent ten years exploring Siberia.

First published by the Imperial Academy of Sciences at St. Petersburg, Müller's *Nouvelle Carte Des Decouvertes etc.* became the primary source for information on the North Pacific until Captain Cook's third voyage. Müller's first map in 1754 was not widely known. In 1758 Müller published a book that contained a revised version. It was translated by Thomas Jefferys and later published in England in 1761.

As the senior naval officer at San Blas on the west coast of Mexico, the Spanish explorer Juan Pérez took copies of two maps by Müller when he was later sent to explore the North Pacific coast by Viceroy Antonio Bucareli in 1774. Mysteriously, information about this first Spanish expedition to British Columbia appeared the following year in an American atlas prepared by Müller's translator, Jefferys, even though the Spanish were highly secretive about their explorations.

BOOKS: Gerhard Friedrich Müller, *Nachricten von Seareisen* (St. Petersburg: 1758) and translated by Carol Furness as *Bering's Voyages: The Reports from Russia by Gerhard Friedrich Müller* (University of Alaska Press, 1986); Gerhard Friedrich Müller, *Voyages from Asia to America, for Completing the Discoveries of the North West Coast of America,* translated by T. Jefferys (London: 1761).

ALEKSEI CHIRIKOV

A leksei Chirikov's first North American landfall north of Dixon Entrance was made approximately 40 nautical miles northwest of Forrester Island, the northernmost land sighted by Spaniard Juan Pérez in 1774—a determining factor in the later negotiations of the maritime border between Alaska and B.C.

Under ominous circumstances, Chirikov also became the first European to encounter indigenous people in the Pacific Northwest on July 24, 1741. The Russian naval commander had sent an eleven-member reconnaissance party ashore in a longboat on July 18 near Lisianki Strait, but they had failed to return. Five days later Chirikov sent a search party of four men in the remaining longboat but they, too, disappeared. Two boats approached the *Paul*, one larger than the other, so Chirikov at first hoped these could be his missing men, but their occupants were paddling, not rowing. The smaller canoe, with four men who were likely Tlingit, came closest to the Russian ship. Hoping to coax them alongside, Chirikov's men waved white kerchiefs, but to no avail. Chirikov recalled, "They stood up and shouted twice, 'Agai, Agai', waved their hands, and turned back to shore." Chirikov crossed the Gulf of Alaska and sighted more than a half-dozen Aleutian Islands, once trading knives for desperately needed food with Aleutian Islanders in kayaks. Of the original 76 men on board, 54 survived.

With encouragement from Empress Catherine the Great, the fur trader Gregory Shelikov began the Russian American Company and established a Russian colony in North America. Shelikov built the first permanent Russian settlement in North America at Kodiak in 1784. There his wife began a school to teach Indians how to speak Russian and to learn the basics of Christianity.

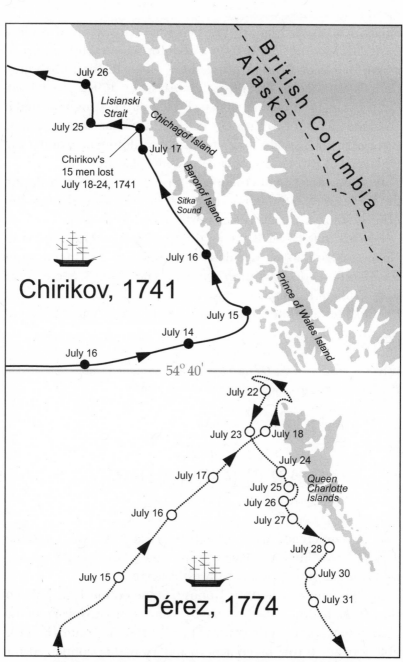

The routes of Russian captain Aleksei Chirikov in 1741 and Spanish explorer
Juan Pérez in 1774 established the present maritime U.S./Canada border.

Shelikov instructed one of his men to erect a series of trading posts "in a southerly direction to California, establishing everywhere marks of Russian possession." The Russian Orthodox Church founded its first mission in Alaska in 1794. A major settlement was attempted at Sitka in 1799, but the Tlingit burned it and killed all but two Russians in 1802. The Russians took their revenge in 1805, establishing their military dominance under the Governor of Russian America, Alexander Baranof.

Russian attempts to create a monopoly in the North Pacific fur trade were ultimately unsuccessful, even though they did briefly establish a trading fort north of San Francisco.

Fearful that Great Britain would overrun its possessions in North America, Russia decided to sell Alaska to the United States for 7.2 million dollars in 1867, as negotiated by U.S. Secretary of State William H. Seward.

Alaska became the 49th sovereign state in the United States of America in 1959.

BOOKS: Vasili A. Divin, *The Great Russian Navigator, A.I. Chirikov,* translated by Raymond H. Fisher (University of Alaska Press, 1993).

ARTHUR DOBBS

As a staunch advocate for increased trade, Arthur Dobbs was a factor in North Pacific exploration because he encouraged the quest to find a Northwest Passage.

To make his case, Arthur Dobbs trumpeted the 1708 publication of the fictional 1640 voyage by a Lima-born Spanish admiral named Bartholomew de Fonte. The report of de Fonte's remarkable journey through a northern waterway that connected the Pacific and Atlantic Oceans, via Hudson Bay, was published in a British magazine called *Memoirs for the Curious.*

Map reputedly drawn for Arthur Dobbs in a London tavern by Joseph La France.

French cartographer Joseph-Nicolas de L'Isle gave further credence to this story when he produced a map in 1752 that credited de Fonte's discoveries. This led, in turn, to Robert de Vaugondy's misleading 1755 map in Diderot's *Encyclopédie* that includes Lac de Fonte. A 1776 map by Venetian Antonio Zatta also represented de Fonte's alleged system of waterways to the Pacific Ocean. This was de Fonte's Strait, the Northwest Passage.

Dobbs also promoted his belief there had to be a Northwest Passage from Hudson's Bay to the Pacific by circulating a map made for him on the floor of a London tavern by Joseph La France, a "French Canadese Indian," who had supposedly journeyed inland through Canada from 1739 to 1742. A Surveyor-General of Ireland, Dobbs lobbied for the abolition of monopolies held by the Hudson's Bay Company on Arctic exploration and the fur trade. He also maintained minerals in the Arctic would one day become more important than beaver pelts. More effectively, Dobbs urged Great Britain increasingly to favour control of exploratory voyages by the Royal Navy, not private interests. Dobbs was naive about geography but his nationalistic arguments were influential due in part to a 1744 publication.

BOOKS: *An Account of the Countries Adjoining to Hudsons Bay* (London, 1744).

DENIS DIDEROT

The French philosopher Denis Diderot's *Encylopédie, ou Dictionnaire Raisonné des Sciences, des Arts et des Métiers*, published in 1755, has been described as perhaps the most extensive gathering of knowledge undertaken in the 18th century. Eventually consisting of 35 volumes, it was banned four years after publication by the king and the church because, with contributions from the likes of Voltaire and Rousseau, its remarkable breadth represented a bulwark or manifesto on behalf of the Enlightenment. Its relevance to British Columbia is slight but not inconsequential.

Diderot and his fellow editors chose to include several maps that were partially based on fabrications, among them Philippe Bauche's *Carte Des Nouvelles Découvertes* and Robert de Vaugondy's map of North America and eastern Asia. The latter map was an

Denis Diderot

embellished copy of a 1752 map made by French geographer Joseph-Nicolas de L'Isle who had returned to France from St. Petersburg after 21 years at the Academy of Sciences. That 1752 map included some reliable details from previously unknown discoveries made by Russian expeditions, but it simultaneously offered a fanciful portrayal of the northwest coast of America derived from the Bartholomew de Fonte hoax now attributed to the short-lived British publication *Memoirs for the Curious* which was published in 1708. This fictional account of de Fonte's voyage referred to a ship from Boston that had navigated into the Pacific via the Northwest Passage. Hence Diderot had an influential role in the quest to find the Northwest Passage that led to the "discovery" of British Columbia.

Nuu-chah-nulth woman as drawn by Tomás de Suría, 1791. Of the 16 groups that comprise the Nuu-chah-nulth First Nation, the Mowachaht band of Gold River traditionally wintered at Tahsis. Others groups include the Ka:'yu:K't'h of Kyuquot; the Ehattesaht of Esperanza Inlet and Zeballos, the Huu-Ay-Aht at Pachena Bay and Cape Beale; the Ahousat on Flores Island, the Tla-o-qui-aht in Clayoquot Sound, the Toquaht of Barkley Sound, the Ucluelet of Ucluelet Inlet, the Uchucklesaht of Uchucklesit Inlet, the Dididaht in the Nitinat Lake region and the Pacheedaht around Port Renfrew. The Tribal Council of the Nuu-chah-nulth is located in Port Alberni—ironically a town named after Pedro de Alberni who led the Spanish contingent of 76 soldiers who arrived in April of 1790 to fortify Friendly Cove under the command of Francisco Eliza.

II
SPANISH

Juan Pérez
Juan Crespi
Tomás de la Peña y Saravia
Bruno de Hezeta
Juan Francisco de la Bodega y Quadra
Francisco Mourelle
José Mariano Moziño
Alejandro Malaspina
Tomás de Suría
Dionisio Alcalá Galiano
Manuel Quimper
Jacinto Caamaño
José Espinosa y Tello

JUAN PÉREZ

History has mostly failed to recognize Juan Pérez for opening the world's last unmapped temperate zone to exploration—and for producing the first map of the British Columbia coast drawn from eyewitness experience. Juan Pérez got here first. Although his ten-month voyage in 1774 has never ranked high in the annals of great maritime achievements because he never landed, Pérez made the first verifiable European contact with British Columbia's indigenous people. His scurvy-ridden voyage was also used to determine the southern boundary of Russian America, giving rise to the 1844 campaign slogan of American presidential candidate James Polk, "54º 40' or Fight!"

The second-in-command was the mercurial Esteban José Martínez, who would instigate the Nootka Crisis in 1789. Both Martínez and Pérez kept diaries. The Martínez entry for July 20 is significant because he notes the presence of "half of a bayonet and...a piece of a sword made into a knife" among the Indians at Santa Margarita. The two diaries were sent to the Viceroy who instructed Melchor de Peramas to make copies. Copies sent to Madrid ended up in the Archivo General de Indias in Seville. The originals ended up in the Archivo General de la Nación in Mexico City. These first reports of British Columbia were ignored for almost two centuries. A doctoral student named Olive Johnson undertook some preliminary translations in 1911 and the Oregon Historical Society arranged for microfilm versions in 1977. Portland historian and researcher Herbert K. Beals finally translated and annotated their publication in 1989.

Not a great deal is known about the first proven European discoverer of British Columbia. Juan Pérez was probably born on the island of Majorca, in Palma, circa 1725. We know his birthday was June 24 because it was celebrated during one of his voyages. Pérez rose to prominence at the naval base in San Blas, Mexico, the Pacific port established by Spain in 1767, and he attained the rank of Pilot First Class by sailing Manila galleons to the Philippines. He also commanded one of the Spanish vessels that reached San Diego in 1769. When Viceroy Antonio María de Bucareli y Ursúa was called upon in 1773 to send a ship north to investigate reports of Russian activity in Alaska, Pérez was the most experienced naval officer available. His instructions were to "not take anything from the Indians against their will, but only in barter or given by them through friendship. All must be treated with kindness and gentleness, which is the efficacious means of gaining and firmly establishing their esteem."

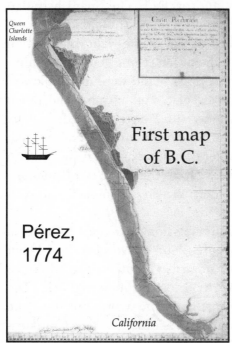

The first coastline map based on exploration was drawn by Juan Pérez's pilot, Joseph de Cañizarez. It includes Monterey in California and the Punta de Santa Magdalena (on the north end of the Queen Charlotte Islands).

Constructed at San Blas, Peréz's ship *Santiago* weighed 225 tons and measured 82 feet long. It embarked on January 24, 1774 carrying 88 officers and men, plus 24 passengers, many of whom were bound for Monterey. The first five months of Pérez's maiden voyage with the *Santiago* were passed in southern California waters, south of San Francisco. The *Santiago* remained in San Diego for structural repairs from March 11 to April 6. It reached Monterey on May 8 and remained there until June 11.

Keeping well out to sea, Pérez became concerned about his

ship's low water supply. He sailed northeast and reached British Columbia on July 18, sighting the northwestern coast of Graham Island, the largest of the Queen Charlotte Islands, also known as Haida Gwaii, just prior to noon. Unable to find a secure harbour to drop anchor, Pérez named the headland Punta Santa de Magdalena. The following afternoon around 4:30 p.m., as Pérez drifted north, three canoes approached. The Spanish traded beads for dried fish. On the following day, 21 Haida canoes appeared, of differing sizes. Two of the canoes had only women and children aboard. "Two of the pagans came aboard the ship," wrote Father Crespi, a Spanish priest, "and were much pleased with the vessel and things on board of it." Father Crespi had joined the Pérez expedition in Monterey with Father Tomás de la Peña y Sarávia. In 1792, the Spaniard Jacinto Caamaño realized that Pérez had approached a smaller island, separated from Graham Island by Parry Passage, and he gave it the name Isla Langara— arguably the birthplace of modern British Columbia because off its shores "first contact" was made.

Pérez named the coastal mountains Los Cerros de San Cristóbal but he never risked going ashore. Pérez sailed north to 54º but was leery of advancing further towards Tlingit territory where he believed the Russian Chirikov had lost his men in 1741. "The Indians told us not to go to that land," he wrote, "for they [the natives there] shot arrows and killed [people]." In fact, Chirikov's crew went ashore almost 200 nautical miles north of where the Spaniards recognized the fragments of a bayonet and swords.

Sailing south, Pérez reached the outskirts of Nootka Sound on the west coast of Vancouver Island on August 7, 1774. The crew's attempt to take ashore a 14-foot cross made by the ship's carpenters was prevented by rising winds. This cross was inscribed with the initials signifying *Jesus Nazarenus Rex Judaeorum*, and it was dated *Carolus Tertius: Rex Hispaniarum; ano 1774*. Anchoring with difficulty near rocks off a small peninsula, Pérez traded with the Nuu-chah-nulth, during which time some silver spoons were allegedly pilfered. These spoons would come to the attention of Captain James Cook four years later upon his landing at Nootka

Sound in 1778. Cook recorded that two spoons were hung around an Indian's neck as ornaments. The purchase of these two spoons by a British seaman was recorded in at least four memoirs that arose from Cook's final voyage. Although there is no record of Pérez's men trading with spoons in 1774, it has been suggested that these spoons might not have been stolen as alleged. They could have been left in the pockets of garments that were exchanged, or simply provided as gifts. Regardless, Spain would cite the spoons as evidence that Spain had preceded the British to British Columbia.

Title page of Juan Pérez's diary, 1774.

In addition to the spoons, Pérez also left behind his anchor. As the weather conditions changed and he found himself in danger of being driven onto the rocks—now called Pérez Rocks—he was unable to raise his anchor. Pérez cut the cable and sailed away, but not before he had named the entrance to Nootka Sound as Rada de San Lorenzo. Pérez named Estevan Point just to the south as La Punta de San Esteban. Estevan Point remains the oldest surviving place name with European origins in British Columbia.

On their return journey, the Spanish might have seen the entrance to the Strait of Juan de Fuca—as Martínez later claimed—but it is certain they saw a prominent mountain on August 11 near Cape Flattery. Pérez named it Cerro de Santa Rosalía. In June of 1788 this was renamed Mount Olympus by John Meares. With his crew threatened by scurvy, Pérez reached Monterey on

August 28, and finally returned to San Blas, much the worse for wear, on November 5.

News of Pérez's voyage came as a disappointment to Spanish authorities because he had sailed only to 54º and 40 minutes north, not 60º north as instructed. Pérez also failed to reassert Spanish dominion for King Carlos III by enacting formal ceremonies of possession, as instructed. Spain had claimed sovereignty over the coastlines of North America ever since Nunez de Balboa crossed the Isthmus of Panama and claimed the Pacific Ocean, and all its shores, in 1513. Pérez did not encounter any Russians and he did not produce detailed charts. His pilot Josef de Cañizárez nonetheless produced a coastline map that included Nootka Sound (*Surgidero de Sn. Lorenzo*), the northern tip of Graham Island (*Pta. de Sta. Margarita*) and Mount Olympus (*Cerro de Sta. Rosalía*).

By 1818, the U.S. and Britain agreed mutually to control the Oregon Territory, a fur-trading region west of the Rocky Mountains between 42º north and 54º and 40 minutes north. The voyage of Pérez was hailed as significant 45 years later—only after the United States, having inherited Spanish claims to sovereignty by virtue of its 1819 Transcontinental Treaty with Spain, argued for greater control of the Pacific Northwest. In 1844, Democratic presidential candidate James Polk adopted the jingoistic motto "54º 40' or Fight!" and threatened to go to war in order to claim all of the Oregon Territory to the southernmost tip of Russian Alaska, where Pérez had reached. The compromise solution that marks the current U.S. border with British Canada was established by the Treaty of Oregon in 1846. A maritime exception to the 49th parallel, whereby the boundary turns south through the Strait of Juan de Fuca, was demarcated in 1872.

In 1981, Brad Merritt of Tsawwassen, bassist for the long-lived Canadian rock band 54•40, chose his music group's unusual numerical name drawn from Polk's American slogan, originating from the Pérez voyage.

Demoted, Pérez sailed north a second time, this time as Pilot for Don Bruno Hezeta's voyage in the *Santiago* in 1775. He died, possibly of typhus, somewhere off the California coast, on November 3, 1775. During the ship's return to San Blas, Pérez was buried at sea.

BOOK: *Juan Pérez on the Northwest Coast: Six Documents of His Expedition in 1774,* translated by H.K. Beals (Portland: Oregon Historical Society Press, 1989).

JUAN CRESPI

One of the four Spaniards among the Pérez expedition to provide the first eyewitness accounts of British Columbia was Father Juan Crespi.

Born in Palma on March 1, 1721, Crespi entered the Franciscan order at age seventeen. He arrived in America in 1749 and made his way to the California peninsula in 1767 where he administered the Mission Purísima Concepción. In 1774, at age fifty-three, Crespi joined the voyage of Juan Pérez. He was probably the oldest man on board. During this voyage Crespi and his fellow priest Tomás de la Peña y Saravia became the first Catholic priests to see British Columbia. Crespi described the first known contacts between Europeans and Indians in British Columbia.

After canoes ventured towards the *Santiago,* he wrote, "While it was still distant from the vessel we heard the people in it singing, and by the intonation we knew they were pagans, for it was the same sung at the dances of pagans from San Diego to Monterey. They were eight men and a boy. Seven of them were paddling; the other, who was advanced in years, was upright and making dancing movements. Throwing several feathers into the sea, they made a turn about the ship."

In describing the second and third canoes that arrived, Crespi noted one of the harpoons had a head of iron "and it looked like that of a boarding-pike." Hence there is more evidence the Haida

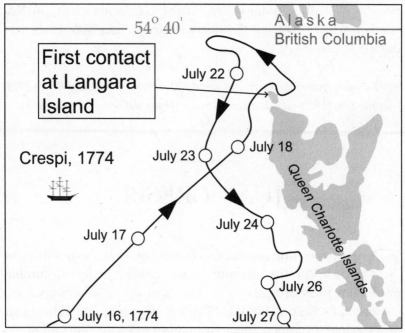

The priest Juan Crespi described meetings with the Haida on July 19, 1774.

had prior contact with mariners from cultures that could produce iron. One of the Spanish mariners accompanying Crespi speculated as much. Later Crespi noted "some pieces of iron and copper and pieces of knives" in the canoes of Hesquiat people off the west coast of Vancouver Island. Captain Cook confirmed such sightings. Crespi reported hearing a "mournful crying out" when the Mowachaht approached the *Santiago* near Nootka. Some 18 years later a Spanish artist named José Moziño visited Nootka Sound and was told by the local Indians that it was thought Pérez's ship had brought a supernatural being named Qua-utz who was coming to punish their misdeeds.

The diaries kept by Crespi and Father Tomás de la Peña y Saravia were handed over to their superior Junípero Serra in Monterey in November 1774. These remained the only two known eyewitness accounts of the Pérez voyage in either Spanish or English for two centuries. The contents of Crespi's diary were first used to supplement a biography of Junípero Serra by Francisco Palóu in 1787. The biographer's transcription of Crespi's diary was later published in full as *Noticias de la Nueva California* in 1857.

Crespi's significant role in British Columbia literary history is little-known and has been overshadowed by his more significant role in California history. In 1769, a Spanish expedition of about 67 men including Crespi, led by Father Junípero Serra and Captain Gaspar de Portola, had entered what is now Los Angeles, by way of Elysian Park, on August 2. Hence Father Juan Crespi was able to record the European origins of Los Angeles.

BOOKS: *Noticias de la Nueva California* (1857) is the Crespi diary as transcribed by Francisco Palóu; edited and translated by G.B. Griffin, *The Journal of Fray Crespi* (Sutro Collection, Los Angeles: Franklin Printing Company, 1891) is the Crespi manuscript dated Oct. 5, 1774; *Fray Juan Crespi: Missionary Explorer on the Pacific Coast, 1769–1774* (University of California Press, 1927; reprinted, New York, AMS Press, 1971) is an English translation of Crespi's journal, edited by Herbert E. Bolton; Donald C. Cutter's *California Coast* (Norman: University of Oklahoma Press, 1969) contains both Crespi and de la Peña diaries.

TOMÁS DE LA PEÑA Y SARAVIA

B orn in northern Spain in 1743, in Brizuela, Tomás de la Peña y Saravia entered the Franciscan order at age nineteen. He joined the Pérez expedition at age thirty-three. His records of the voyage are sometimes more detailed than those of Juan Crespi. Along with Pérez and Crespi, Tomás de la Peña y Saravia documented sightings of fair-haired, blue-eyed Haida in 1774.

The long-held notion that some sailors from Francis Drake's *Golden Hind* might have visited the Haida in the late 16th century was enhanced by a portrait of the Haida chief Cunnyha (among various spellings) painted by Sigismund Bacstrom in 1792 or the spring of 1793. As a sailor on one of two British fur trading ships,

Butterworth and *Three Brothers,* Bacstrom depicted the blue-eyed Haida near Langara Island where the Spanish priests aboard *Santiago* had seen them about 20 years earlier.

BOOK: *California Coast* (Norman: University of Oklahoma Press, 1969) by Donald C. Cutter contains both Crespi and Peña diaries.

—————

BRUNO DE HEZETA

"The Spaniards were obsessed by this idea that they didn't want to give away state secrets."
—GLYNDWR WILLIAMS, HISTORIAN, UNIVERSITY OF LONDON

Bruno de Hezeta y Dudagoitia was the second European captain to make contact with Indians within the boundaries of present-day British Columbia. He met Indians off the southern end of Vancouver Island in 1775.

Hezeta also made the first map of the Washington state coastline, taking formal possession of the area for Spain, and he was the first European to record evidence of the mouth of the Columbia River. On August 17, 1775, Hezeta wrote, "These currents and seething of the waters have led me to believe that it may be the mouth of some great river or some passage to another sea." Spain chose not to publish information about his voyage and his accomplishments are little-known.

Among some scholars, Hezeta has also gained the dubious distinction of leading the first expedition that could have brought smallpox to the Pacific Northwest, thereby eradicating approximately 30 percent of the population of Puget Sound tribes during the 1770s. In his book, *In The Coming of the Spirit of Pestilence,* historian Robert Boyd estimated that smallpox in the 1770s killed more than 11,000 Western Washington Indians, reducing the area's population from about 37,000 to 26,000.

An "aged informant" from the Squamish tribe told Charles Hill-Tout in the 1890s about another plague. Hill-Tout then wrote, "[A] dreadful misfortune befell them.... One salmon season the fish were found to be covered with running sores and blotches, which rendered them unfit for food. But as the people depended very largely upon these salmon for their winter's food supply, they were obliged to catch and cure them as best they could, and store them away for food. They put off eating them till no other food was available, and then began a terrible time of sickness and distress. A dreadful skin disease, loathsome to look upon, broke out upon all alike. None were spared. Men, women, and children sickened, took the disease and died in agony by hundreds, so that when the spring arrived and fresh food was procurable, there was scarcely a person left of all their numbers to get it. Camp after camp, village after village, was left desolate. The remains of which, said the old man, in answer to my queries on this, are found today in the old camp sites or midden-heaps over which the forest has been growing for so many generations."

Hezeta had been sent in the *Santiago*, with Juan Franscisco de la Bodega y Quadra in the *Sonora*, to reach 65º north to investigate possible Russian incursions. Viceroy Bucareli had placed Hezeta in command of the *Santiago* because Juan Pérez had failed precisely to follow instructions—but Hezeta did not fully complete his assignment either. Using Jacques Nicolas Bellin's 1766 map, Hezeta's crew reached the Olympic Peninsula in July, stopping near present-day Point Grenville, where some of Quadra's men were killed by Indians when they went ashore for water.

Beset by scurvy or some unknown disease aboard the *Santiago*, Hezeta sailed north to 50º. He then became separated from the *Sonora* in rough seas and headed south where he met some Indians off the coast of Vancouver Island.

Encountering swirling tides near the mouth of the Columbia River, Hezeta wondered if he had found the strait that Juan de Fuca had reported, the one that could lead the Spanish to the hoped-for Sea of the West. Most of his crew were so ill that Hezeta was unable to drop anchor and investigate but he made the first map of the Columbia River estuary. The area near the Columbia River estuary appeared on some Spanish maps as Entrada de Hezeta but Robert Gray is usually credited with finding the river. The journal of the priest travelling with Hezeta, Miguel de la Campos Cos, was published in 1964 as *A Journal of Explorations Northward Along the Coast from Monterey in the Year 1775*, edited by John Galvin (San Francisco: John Howell Books, 1964).

BOOKS: *For Honor & Country: The Diary of Bruno de Hezeta*, translation and annotation by Herbert K. Beals (Portland: Western Imprints, 1985; Oregon Historical Society Press, 2000).

CAPTAIN BODEGA Y QUADRA

"I pressed on, taking fresh trouble for granted."
— JUAN FRANCISCO DE LA BODEGA Y QUADRA, 1775

As early as 1527, Spanish galleons sailed between Mexico and the Philippines. By 1564, Captain Alonso de Arellano confirmed that westerly winds in the Pacific could allow for annual cross-Pacific voyages. During a voyage from Manila to Acapulco, a Spanish galleon named *San Francisco Xavier* was shipwrecked on the Oregon coast, near Nehalem Beach, in 1707, but for the most part Spain was content to leave the North Pacific unexplored. That is, until Madrid learned about the incursions of Russian traders into their great "Spanish lake."

Don Juan Francisco de la Bodega y Quadra, or simpy Quadra, is the best-known of the many Spanish captains who reached the coast of British Columbia. Born in Lima, Peru, on May 22, 1744, he graduated as a midshipman from the Naval Academy in Cádiz, Spain, in 1767 and arrived in New Spain in 1774. The following year he led the second Spanish naval voyage to sail as far as British Columbia and the first to claim sovereignty over Alaska.

Initially Bruno de Hezeta had commanded the *Santiago*, with Bruno Hecate as his pilot—after whom Hecate Sound is named—while Quadra was placed aboard the *Sonora* under Captain Don Juan Manuel de Ayala. Quadra was given command of the *Sonora* after the captain of a third ship accompanying them as far as San Francisco Bay reportedly went mad, causing Ayala to switch ships. Francisco Mourelle became Quadra's pilot.

In July, their crew encountered violent resistance on the Washington State coast when seven Spanish/Mexican sailors were massacred by more than 200 Indians at a place they called Punta de los Mártires, now believed to be Port Grenville. Quadra and Mourelle persisted in their tiny schooner, despite scurvy and a reluctant crew, making realistic charts as far as Kruzov Island, Sitka Sound and Bucareli Bay on Prince of Wales Island, sailing as far north as 58°.

North of Sitka, the Spanish found a crudely constructed shelter where they erected the first Spanish cross on the coast of the Pacific Northwest. Not encountering any Russians, the Spanish formally declared Spanish sovereignty over the northern coast in the name of Carlos III, King of Spain and the West Indies. They conducted a Christian ceremony on August 18, 1775, at Salisbury Sound, Alaska, a place named Puerto de los Remedios by the Spanish. Mourelle oversaw these ceremonies because his captain was ill. Today Quadra is mainly remembered in B.C. for his later voyage that resulted in a famous meeting with Captain George Vancouver at Nootka Sound.

Three years later, in 1778, Captain James Cook arrived at

Nootka Sound on the Pacific coast to take possession of "territories useful" to England, but the Spaniards were still unaware of Cook's achievement when Quadra undertook his second voyage north, with two frigates, in 1779. Again sailing from San Blas with Mourelle, Quadra and his associate commander Ignacio de Artega reached as far north as Prince William Sound, Cook Inlet and Kodiak Island in Alaska before turning back due to illness.

Quadra's most crucial role as a diplomat in British Columbia was yet to come.

After Esteban José Martínez's arrival at Friendly Cove on May 5, 1789, the Spanish set to work building a fort under his direction. He was soon troubled by the arrival of Captain James Colnett's ship bringing Chinese labourers. Martínez arrested Colnett and seized two other English ships, taking control for Spain on June 14, 1789. This was the famous Nootka Incident.

When Martínez was aboard one of the English ships, Chief Callicum, son-in-law of the Mowachaht Chief Maquinna, came alongside in a canoe, seemingly shouting accusations that Martínez was a thief. Infuriated, Martínez fired his musket. It malfunctioned but a nearby Spanish soldier also fired, murdering Callicum. This killing, whether accidental or deliberate, according to Quadra's biographer Freeman M. Tovell, "was a black cloud that hung over the Spanish for the entire five years of their presence."

The Spanish prevailed and built a tiny fort or "presidio," as instructed, to feign permanent Spanish control. This was the first Spanish establishment on Canada's West Coast, and the first attempt at permanent European settlement. Tovell has pointed out the Spanish settlement was dependent upon Chief Maquinna, who used the Spanish to assert his own superiority among rival chiefs. "There was no formal cession of the land to Spain and no part of it was donated or sold," writes Tovell in *BC Historical News*, Vol. 34, No. 4, of 2001, "Occupancy was based solely on Chief Maquinna's verbal consent beginning with Martínez in 1789, ratified with Francisco de Eliza in 1790 and Alejandro Malaspina during the latter's brief visit in 1791, and confirmed to Bodega y

With the approval of Chief Ambrose Maquinna, this stained glass window appears
in the church erected at Yuquot (Friendly Cove) by the government of Spain.
It depicts the meeting between Captain George Vancouver and Commander
Bodega y Quadra in 1792 to resolve territorial disputes in accordance with the
Nootka Convention of 1790. Subsequent Nootka Conventions were signed in 1793
and 1794. In 1795, the Spanish dismantled their fort at Nootka. The other stained glass
window in the church depicts Padre Magin Catala, the first Spanish missionary at
Friendly Cove in 1793. A seldom-seen, overgrown grave in the woods still marks his
burial. With its lettering covered by thick moss, the fenced marble tombstone once had
a prominent place beside a Catholic school that the Mowachaht—including Yuquot
caretakers Ray and Terry Williams—attended in the early 20th century.

Quadra in 1792."

The apprehension of Colnett by Martínez at Nootka Sound led to serious diplomatic exchanges between London and Madrid. On October 28, 1790, Spain and England signed the first Nootka Convention providing for mutual territorial rights and mutual access. Each country named commissioners to oversee the loose terms of the truce. They were Captain George Vancouver and Captain Bodega y Quadra.

Caretaker Ray Williams uncovers the tombstone of the first Catholic missionary at Friendly Cove.

In 1789, Bodega y Quadra had been appointed as commander of the San Blas naval department. To reassert the Spanish pre-eminence, Quadra drew his "Carta General de quanto esta hoy se ha descubierto y examinado por los Españoles en la Costa Septemtional de California" in 1791. This was a general map showing how far north the Spaniards had explored north of Acapulco. Captain Bodega y Quadra then sailed north for his famous meeting with Captain George Vancouver at Yuquot, at the entrance of Nootka Sound, in 1792.

Bodega y Quadra arrived on April 29, well-prepared, with three ships, the *Activa*, *Princesa* and *Santa Gertrudis*, and an English interpreter, Félix Cepeda. The Vancouver expedition did not arrive until August 28. Vancouver lacked an interpreter and detailed instructions but the two men had cordial relations, writing letters back and forth for translation. By all accounts Bodega y

Quadra was an impressive diplomat. "I constantly treat Maquinna as a friend," the Spaniard wrote, "singling him out among all with the clearest demonstrations of esteem. He always occupies the place of honour at my table and I take myself the trouble to serve him." This much impressed Captain Vancouver. "I could not help observing," Vancouver wrote, "with a mixture of surprise and pleasure how much the Spaniards had succeeded in gaining the good opinion and confidence of the people; together with the very orderly behaviour, so conspicuously evident in their conduct towards the Spaniards on all occasions."

During Bodega y Quadra's four months at Nootka, his diplomacy and friendship with Maquinna prevented an uprising that was planned by the rival chiefs Wickaninnish, Tatoosh and Cleaskinah (aka "Captain Hanna"), the chief of the Ahousat. When Maquinna prevailed upon one of the malcontents, Hannah, to come to Yuquot and meet Bodega y Quadra, the Spanish captain was so persuasively charming that Hannah decided to forego plans for an uprising. "These people can never expect to have among them a better friend than Don Quadra," observed the American fur trader Joseph Ingraham, master of the *Hope*. "Nothing can exceed his attention and kindness to them, and they all seem sensible of it and are extravagantly fond of him." In short, Bodega y Quadra set a standard by which other Europeans would be judged.

In the company of their host Chief Maquinna, Quadra and Vancouver amicably agreed to call the island "the Island of Quadra and Vancouver" but they were unable to clarify the terms of the Nootka Convention. Instead, they opted to defer intricate negotiations to their respective governments.

Captain Vancouver wrote, "The well known generosity of my other Spanish friends, will, I trust, pardon the warmth of expression with which I must ever advert to the conduct of Señor Quadra; who, regardless of the difference of opinion that had risen between us in our diplomatic capacities at Nootka, had uniformly maintained toward us a character infinitely beyond the reach of my powers of encomium to describe. His benevolence was not only confined to the common rights of hospitality, but was extended to all occasions, and was exercised in every instance, where His Majesty's service, combined with my commission, was in the least concerned."

Quadra left Nootka Sound in the *Princesa* in late September. The need to resolve the English/Spanish territorial dispute subsided as European powers came to accept there was not any viable sea passage from the north Pacific to the Atlantic. As well, an over-supply of sea otter furs glutted the market in the Orient, reducing prices. England and Spain signed another agreement on January 11, 1794, that relieved diplomatic tensions.

The Nootka presidio built by the Spanish was dismantled on March 23, 1795, marking the end of Spanish dominance on the West Coast of Canada.

The last Spanish voyage north of California would be made by Juan Tovar in the schooner *Sutil* in 1796. Some other Spanish maritime explorers who followed in Quadra's wake include José María Narváez, Gonzalo López de Haro, Cayetano Valdés y Bazán, Lieutenant Francisco de Eliza, José Verdía, Juan Pantoja, Alonso de Torres, Juan Martínez Zayas and Lieutenant Salvador Fidalgo.

Captain Bodega y Quadra died at San Blas in 1794. Quadra Island was named for him in 1903. Something of his complex nature is revealed in his comment, "I flatter myself that by treating these Indians as people should be treated and not as though they are individuals of an inferior nature, I have lived in complete tranquillity."

BOOKS: Copies of Bodega y Quadra's journal have been found in the archives of the Ministerio de Asuntos Exteriores in Madrid and within the Revilla Gigedo Papers belonging to Irving W. Robbins. Publications include *Juan Francisco de la Bodega y Quadra: el descubrimiento del fin del mundo,* editado por Salvador Bernabeu *(Madrid: Alianza Editorial, 1990)* and *Nutka 1792, Viaje a la Costa N.O. de la América Septentrional por Don Juan Francisco de la Bodega y Quadra, del orden de Santiago, Capitán de Navio...y Comandante del Departamento de San Blas en las fragatas de sumando Santa Gertrudis, Aránzazu, Princesa y Goleta Activo, año de 1792,* eds. Palau, Mercedes & F. Tovell, P. Spratz, R. Inglis (Madrid, 1998).

FRANCISCO MOURELLE

"Both sexes exhibited docility and agreeableness."
—MOURELLE SUMMARIZING CONTACTS WITH HAIDA IN 1774

An English translation of Francisco Mourelle's 1775 journal mysteriously appeared in 1781 amid Daines Barrington's compilation of scientific articles entitled *Miscellanies*. It is not known how a copy of Mourelle's navigation journal was acquired for English translation. It rivals John Rickman's journal as the earliest account of British Columbia to appear in English.

Francisco A. Mourelle de la Rúa (1750–1820) served as naviga-tor for Bodega y Quadra's first two voyages north in 1775 and 1779. Later, in 1791, he was assigned the task of compiling records pertaining to the 1774 voyage of Juan Pérez. Despite failing health, Mourelle was conducting an overview of all Spanish maritime activity on the Pacific Coast for the Viceroy Conde de Revillagigedo. With-out having sailed with Pérez, Mourelle pre-pared a summary of the Pérez voyage and a "Tabla Diaria" that lists all latitudes and longitudes for each day of the voyage.

Describing the first contact between Spaniards and Haida in 1774, Mourelle transcribed the reactions of Pérez as: "It was then observed that they were of robust stature, cheerful in appear-ance, with beautiful eyes and handsome faces. The hair consisted of a queue, although some simply had it tied up. They have beards in the manner of the Chinese; they are white in color, and many of them have blue eyes. The women are good looking; they have the lower lip perforated, in which incision is inserted an object that is a different size depending on whether [the wearer] is young or old; it appeared that only the married ones had them. Both sexes exhibited docility and agreeableness; the women were dressed in pelt tunics fitted to the body, with bracelets of copper or iron, and rings of the same metals."

Mourelle's evidence of the first Spanish visit to B.C. is housed in the Bancroft Library in Berkeley. The National Library of Canada has a copy of Mourelle's 1781 memoir of his time with Bodega y Quadra. Mourelle is also the subject of a 1978 book in Spanish by Amancio Landín Carrasco. The Maurelle Islands in Alaska and Maurelle Island in the Inside Passage are named after him although Mourelle is the correct spelling of his name.

BOOKS: *Miscellanies* (London: J. Nichols, 1781) by Daines Barrington inexplicably contains Francisco Mourelle's translated memoir entitled *Journal of a Voyage in 1775 to Explore the Coast of America Northward of California, by the Second Pilot of the Fleet, Don Francisco Antonio Maurelle [i.e. Mourelle] in the King's Schooner Called the Sonora and Commanded by Don Juan Francico de la Bodega* . It is one of the earliest published memoirs of the Pacific Northwest.

First page of Mourelle's Tabla Diaria that chronicles each day of Pérez's 1774 voyage.

JOSÉ MARIANO MOZIÑO

*"One of the most conspicuous scientific personalities that
New Spain produced in the eighteenth century."*
—MEXICAN HISTORIAN ALBERTO M. CARREÑO

*"We are indebted to Mosiño for almost all the knowledge and
accounts that we possess in regard to the inhabitants of Nootka."*
—LIEUTENANT ALCALÁ GALIANO

The first important scientist in B.C. was the botanist José
Mariano Moziño. He accompanied Bodega y Quadra to
Nootka Sound and wrote the most comprehensive Spanish book
pertaining to B.C. in the 18th century, *Noticias de Nutka: An Account of Nootka Sound in 1792*, completed in 1793. It is the first
work of anthropology pertaining to British Columbia.

"Our residence of more than four months on that island," he
wrote, "enabled me to learn about the various customs of the
natives, their religion, and their system of government. I believe
I am the first person who has been able to gather such information, and this was because I learned their language sufficiently to
converse with them."

Although Moziño probably exaggerated his ability to learn the
language in a matter of months, his immersion in Nuu-chah-
nulth culture greatly assisted the Spanish in gaining the upper
hand in their dealings with Chief Maquinna during the period
of the Nootka Crisis.

Moziño was sufficiently adept at languages to glean the following verification of Pérez's preceding visit to San Lorenzo (Nootka
Sound) in 1774. "The sight of the ship at first filled the natives
with terror, and even now they testify that they were seized with

75

fright from the moment they saw on the horizon the giant "machine" which little by little approached their coasts. They believed that Qua-utz [the creator] was coming to make a second visit, and were fearful that it was in order to punish the misdeeds of the people. As many as were able hid themselves in the mountains, others closed themselves up in their lodges, and the most daring took their canoes out to examine more closely the huge mass that had come out of the ocean. They approached it timorously, without sufficient courage to go aboard, until after awhile, attracted by the friendly signs by which the Spanish crew called them, they boarded the ship and inspected with wonder all the new and extraordinary objects that were presented to them. They received a number of gifts and in return gave the captain some otter skins."

Moziño noted that Nootka was not an Indian word and supposed Captain Cook had misinterpreted the word *Nut-chi*, meaning mountain. He was also the first of many to mention the practice of polygamy among Northwest Coast Indians and to report on birth practices, fertility and sexuality. "As soon as they throw off the afterbirth, they run into the sea and swim with great resolution. What is strange is that after a son is born, if his father is a *tais* [meaning chief], he has to enclose himself in the lodge, seeing neither the sun nor the waves. He is fearful of gravely offending *Qua-utz*, who would leave both him and his son without life in punishment of his sin.... Names are changed according to one's age, and in this matter each new one is solemnized with greater luxury and magnificence than the first one.... As soon as the menstrual flow appears in a girl for the first time, they celebrate in the same manner, and her name is also changed. If by chance she is the daughter of the principal chief of the *taises*, this proclamation occurs on the same day. We were present to congratulate Maquinna for that of his daughter Izto-coti-clemot, who before this time was called Apenas."

Moziño was born of Spanish parents in Temascaltepec, Mexico in 1757. He was admitted to the Seminario Tridentino in Mexico City in 1774. He received his degree in scholastic theology and

Title page of Moziño's Noticias de Nutka *from the manuscript found in Mexico City.*

ethics at age twenty and married Doña Rita Rivera y Melo Montaño in 1778. He moved to Oaxaca as a professor and seminarian. Dissatisfied with teaching in a provincial atmosphere, he returned to Mexico City to complete his studies in medicine at the Pontifical University, simultaneously studying mathematics at the Royal Academy of San Carlos. He excelled in all fields, first earning a Bachelor of Medicine in 1787, then enrolling in courses in botany at the Royal Botanical Garden where he became the outstanding student of the year. With his classmate José Maldonado, he collected and named hundreds of species of plants for Martín Sessé, director of the Royal Scientific Expedition to New Spain. He and Maldonado and the artist Atanasio Echeverría were selected to join the expedition of Captain Bodega y Quadra that reached Nootka Sound on April 29, 1792.

Moziño frankly described the nature of relations between the Spanish and the Nuu-chah-nulth, recording how the Spanish "insulted them at various times, crippled some and wounded others, and did not fail to kill several." Ahousat Nuu-chah-nulth elder Peter Webster has corroborated the brutal treatment of sex workers in *Sound Heritage* VII-2. "They used to pull them into the blacksmith's without any romance," he said. "The blacksmith had that red-hot iron always ready for those who refused."

A Spanish astronomer reported by 1792 that "the natives are already beginning to experience the terrible ravages of syphilis, which threatens them with the appalling fate which overtook the ancient inhabitants of California, a race which has become almost extinct owing to this disease."

Based on his visit to Vancouver Island for six months in 1792, Moziño's study was augmented by the first Nootka-Spanish dictionary, catalogues of plants and animals, and paintings by Atanasio Echeverría.

A copy of his manuscript—not the missing original—was recovered from the Sociedad Mexicana's library in 1880, without drawings, and was republished in 1913 with a minimal print run. It remained long ignored by scholars in English. A few other copies are now known to exist in Paris, Madrid, Yale University Library and a private collection. The Yale manuscript version is entitled *Relación de la Isla de Mazarredo* and has been footnoted and altered by a scribe. The published 1913 version from Mexico City was translated and edited by Iris Higbie Wilson, a San Diego historian, with various illustrations added.

Formally trained in medicine, theology and botany, José Mariano Moziño also wrote on medical and philosophical subjects. Co-written with his mentor Martín Sessé, Moziña's *Flora Mexicana* (1885) and *Plantae Novae Hispaniae* (1889) were published by the Sociedad Mexicana de Historia Natural.

Moziño was employed by the Royal Scientific Expedition in Mexico, Guatemala and the West Indies until 1803, at which time he travelled to Madrid with Sessé. Unfortunately King Carlos IV lacked his father's regard for the importance of natural history.

France invaded Spain in 1808, forcing Carlos IV to abdicate in favour of his son. When the French took Madrid, Napoleon's brother Joseph Bonaparte appointed the hitherto under-appreciated Moziño as the director of the Royal Museum of Natural History as well as professor of zoology at the Royal Academy of Medicine. These favours were short-lived.

Upon the French withdrawal from Spain, Moziño was arrested by patriots as a traitor. He fled on foot to the French border. His precious manuscripts, drawings and herbaria were transferred to a handcart. He eventually reached Montpellier where Swiss scientist Augustin-Pyramus de Candolle recognized the value of his 1400 drawings of plants and animals. In 1816 Moziño had to refuse the Swiss offer to go to Geneva and classify his work, saying, "No, I am too old and sick; I am too unfortunate; take them to Geneva; I give them to you, and I entrust to your care my future glory."

In 1792, Moziño recorded the coming-of-age (menstruation) celebration for Chief Maquinna's daughter Izto-coti-clemot, formerly Apenas.

Moziño was granted permission to return to Spain in 1817. He contacted Candolle and asked for the return of his work. The Swiss botanist quickly hired artists to copy 860 sketches in eight days, in addition to making 119 rough drafts. This proved providential. Moziño died in Barcelona in May of 1820. His original drawings have long since disappeared, but the precise copies made in Switzerland remain.

BOOKS: *Noticias de Nutka* (Gazeta de Guatemala, 1803 Volume VII, 1804 Volume VIII); *Noticias de Nutka,* ed. Alberto M. Carreño (Sociedad Mexicana de Geografía, 1913); *Noticias de Nutka: An Account of Nootka Sound in 1792,* translated and edited by Iris Higbie Engstrand (McClelland & Stewart, 1970; reprinted by University of Washington Press in 1991).

<hr>

ALEJANDRO MALASPINA

"Who's heard of Malaspina? The tragedy of his voyage was that this enormous mass of material he gathered did not come out at the time."
—GLYNDWR WILLIAMS, HISTORIAN

The great under-appreciated explorer of the Pacific Northwest was Alejandro Malaspina, born within the boundaries of present-day Italy, who rivalled Captains Bodega y Quadra, Cook and Vancouver as one of the most remarkable men to visit the Pacific Northwest in the late 18th century.

Born in northern Tuscany, at Mulazzo, in the Spanish-held Duchy of Parma, on November 5, 1754, Alejandro Malaspina was the second son of the Count of Malaspina. He was christened Alexandro Malaspina but later adopted an alternate spelling of his first name. During the 1760s he lived for several years with his family in Palermo in the home of his great-uncle Giovanni Fogliani Szorza d'Aragona, the viceroy of Sicily. Malaspina was educated in Rome at the Clementine College, managed by the Somaschi Fathers, from 1765 to 1773. Accepted into the Order of Malta, he spent a year in Malta learning the fundamentals of sailing prior to entering the Royal Navy in 1774. He participated in various Spanish battles and sailed to the Philippines, rising in rank until he was denounced to the Court of the Inquisition in

Alejandro Malaspina

1782, suspected of heresy. These accusations were not upheld and he continued to distinguish himself in the navy, participating in the Spanish attack on Gibraltar and making a second voyage to the Philippines, this time as second-in-command, in 1783–1784. He undertook cartography surveys on the Spanish coast in 1785, then he sailed from September 1786 to May 1788 in the frigate *Astrea* on behalf of the Royal Philippine Company, navigating by way of the Cape of Good Hope and returning around Cape Horn.

In 1788, Malaspina's ambitious nature was evidenced by his proposal for a two-ship expedition to visit almost all of Spain's Asian and American territories, in concert with José de Bustamante y Guerra (1759–1825). This "Plan for a Scientific and Political Voyage Around the World" would ideally bring as much glory to Spain as Captain Cook's voyages had given England. Malaspina was an intense rationalist who held the position of Associate Correspondent of the Royal

Academy of Sciences in Turin. Whereas Cook's voyages had yielded a three-volume report, Malaspina would aim for an eight-volume omnibus.

With José de Bustamante y Guerra, Malaspina sailed from Cádiz on July 30, 1789 in the *Descubierta* (the Discovery) and the *Atrevida* (the Daring). These two corvettes, built especially for the expedition, were named by Malaspina in honour of James Cook's *Discovery* and *Resolution*. Throughout the second half of 1789 and all of 1790, Malaspina and his crews gathered extensive scientific and ethnographic information while visiting Spanish American territories that included Montevideo, Port Egmont, Valparaiso, Callao, Guayaquil and Panamá. The expedition's artists would later include José Cardero and Tomás de Suría.

Unfortunately for Malaspina, his thoroughness contributed to his undoing. Prior to embarkation he had sent José Espinosa y Tello to conduct research into all preceding Pacific voyages. Espinosa had uncovered a copy of Lorenzo Ferrer Maldonado's *Relación* of 1609 that contained a bogus account of an alleged voyage, via Davis Strait, to the Strait of Anian. Malaspina rightly dismissed this account and set about his high-minded task, sailing with an unprecedented assortment of scientists, and the latest surveying and navigational equipment. But upon reaching Acapulco in March of 1791, Malaspina received new orders from the King of Spain. Instead of heading west to the Hawaiian Islands, Malaspina was told to sail north in search of the Strait of Anian, based on the Maldonado material uncoverd by Espinosa.

Whereas Cook's crews were necessarily loyal in hostile territories, Malaspina's men could leave their jobs much more easily during frequent visits to Spanish enclaves. More than a dozen of Malaspina's men deserted at Acapulco upon learning they were not bound for Hawaii. Malaspina, a skeptic, resented the "wild-goose chase" to explore the coast between 59º and 60º north but he dutifully sailed into the Alaskan waters already visited by Captains George Dixon and Cook. He reached Port Mulgrave and mapped Yakutat Bay, and would later examine the coast as far north as Prince William Sound.

This Gabriola Island rock formation is still known as Malaspina Gallery.

The artist Tomás de Suría reported great excitement at the end of June when, much to Malaspina's surprise, their expedition discovered an apparent opening that might be the long-sought inlet to the east. Two launches, provisioned for 15 days, were sent to investigate the potential continental passage on July 2, only to return almost immediately, stymied by the looming presence of the Hubbard Glacier. The inlet was a cul-de-sac of ice. Malaspina took formal possession of the glacial area for Spain, made detailed hydrographical surveys, and recorded valuable ethnographic information about his meetings with the Tlingit. Malaspina called the place Deception Bay.

Detoured by Maldonado's artifice, Malaspina, a meticulous surveyor, blamed speculative scholars for continuing to hamper the efforts of practical mariners such as himself. Ironically the explorer most leery of non-scientific maps had been victimized by them. Discouraged, Malaspina sailed south in August to Nootka Sound, spending a month with Chief Maquinna and the Mowachaht at Yuquot (at which time Tomás de Suría made his famous pencil portrait of Maquinna). Here Malaspina's longboats explored Nootka Sound's channels. Navigational charts made by Malaspina while anchored at Nootka were among the nine Spanish maps that were later provided to George Vancouver.

At Nootka, Malaspina and his officers wrote extensive reports about the Spanish garrison and the Mowachaht, and described Chief Maquinna: "The character of Maquinna is difficult to decipher. His personality seems simultaneously fierce, suspicious and intrepid. The natural tendency of his inclinations is probably much disturbed on one hand by the desire of the Europeans to cultivate his friendship, the treasure he has accumulated in a few years and the discord between the Europeans themselves, and perhaps their attempts to obtain a monopoly of the fur trade; and on the other hand, the weakness of his forces, the skirmishes suffered, the usefulness of the trade, and the too frequent presence of European ships in these parts."

Malaspina headed south to Monterey, San Blas and Acapulco, reporting his failure to find the Strait of Anian. He headed across the Pacific in December, reaching Guam, and proceeded to the Philippines where his men passed nine months making extensive reports. Bustamante sailed in the *Atrevida* to Macao to make gravitational observations. After 62 months at sea, Malaspina's expedition returned to Cádiz on September 21, 1794. During his five years abroad, Malaspina had written 450,000 words in his journal. He was received by King Charles IV and Prime Minister Manuel Godoy in December, then promoted to fleet-brigadier, but Malaspina's progressive nature and liberal proposals were soon at odds with Godoy. Foreseeing the potential value of the British Columbia coast, Malaspina counselled Madrid to settle the area. A liberal before his time, Malaspina also suggested Spain ought to dispense with military domination and establish a confederation of free trading states, a Pacific Rim trading block that could be managed from Acapulco.

Malaspina's downfall was a letter he sent to the Queen suggesting Godoy ought to be replaced. When Godoy learned of this opposition, Malaspina was arrested in November of 1795 for plotting against the state. After an inconclusive trial, he was imprisoned in northern Spain, sequestered in a remote castle from 1796 to 1802. While confined, Malaspina remained active as a writer on subjects that included economics, literature and aesthetics. Napoleon and Francesco Melzi d'Eril successfully lobbied for his release in 1802. He was freed on condition that he would leave Spain. Malaspina travelled from Genoa to his hometown of Mulazzo in March of 1803, settling in nearby Pontremoli where he took an active interest in civic affairs. Malaspina was entrusted with organizing a response to an outbreak of yellow fever and later appointed Advising Auditor of the Council of State of the Kingdom of Italy in 1805. He received further honours, including the title of Addomesticato, to the Columban Society in Florence, prior to his death in Pontremoli on April 9, 1810.

Malaspina's magnificent journal was suppressed during his lifetime. A subsidiary portion appeared in 1802 but all mention of Malaspina was expunged. The complete text of his five-year report was not published in Spanish until 1885. A three-volume edition has been translated for the Hakluyt Society in association with the Museo Naval, with the final volume dealing with the northwest coast. A Spanish biography of Malaspina by Dario Manfredi, translated by Teresa and Don Kirchner, has been made available on the internet and Vancouver's John Kendrick published a biography in 1999. Malaspina's political writings, most notably *Axiomas políticos sobre la América*, are being translated.

In deference to Malaspina's enlightened character and his largely unheralded pursuits in physics, astronomy and political philosophy, Malaspina University-College in Nanaimo has been named in his honour. As directed by Malaspina, the schooners *Sutíl* and *Mexicana* under Captains Dionisio Alcalá Galiano and Cayetano Valdés explored the Georgia and Juan de Fuca Straits, an expedition that gave rise to the name of Malaspina Strait between Texada Island and the Sechelt Peninsula—even though Malaspina had never entered the Strait of Georgia. The Alexandro Malaspina Research Centre was created at the Malaspina University-College in Nanaimo in 1999.

BOOKS: *Salvá (Miguel) y Baranda (Pedro Sainz de), Colección de documentos inéditos, etc., 8°, Vol. XV* (Madrid, 1849); *La Expedición Malaspina 1789-1794, Diario General del Viaje por Alejandro Malaspina, Tomo II — Vol. I & II* (Ministerio de Defensa, Museo Naval, Madrid, 1991); *The Malaspina Expedition 1789-1794, The Journal of the Voyage of Alejandro Malaspina, Vol I. Cádiz to Panamá,* edited by Andrew David, Felipe Fernández-Armesto, Carlos Novi & Glyndwr Williams (London: Hakluyt Society, third series, no. 8, 2001); *The Malaspina Expedition 1789-1794, The Journal of the Voyage of Alejandro Malaspina, Vol II. Panamá to the Philippines,* edited by Andrew David, Felipe Fernández-Armesto, Carlos Novi & Glyndwr Williams (London: Hakluyt Society, third series, no. 10, 2003). Also see bibliography section for Malaspina.

TOMÁS DE SURÍA

"It [Suría's journal] possesses the freshness and naiveté of a landlubber afloat." —HISTORIAN DONALD C. CUTTER

Also known as Tomás de Surís, the artist Tomás de Suría accompanied Alejandro Malaspina during the northwest coast section of his voyage of scientific discovery from 1789 to 1795. At Nootka Sound he described the Spanish practice of trading guns for children who were slaves, ostensibly to baptize them and save them from alleged cannibalism. "There was one among them whom the sailors called Primo.... He told us that he had been destined to be a victim and to be eaten by Chief Macuina together with many others, and that this custom was practiced with the younger prisoners of war, as well as in the ceremonies which were used in such a detestable and horrible sacrifice."

Others who gathered knowledge for the Malaspina expedition included chief scientist Antonio Piñeda, the French-born botanist Luis Née and naturalist Tadeo Haenke from Prague. Haenke had remarkable abilities as a linguist, musician, physician, minerologist, botanist and chemist. The two astronomers José Espinosa y Tello and Ciriaco Zevallos are immortalized in the place names for the Vancouver Island town of Zeballos and nearby Espinoza Inlet.

The other artist to visit the North Pacific with Malaspina was José Cardero, the cabin boy from Ecija in southern Spain. Malaspina had originally hired two Spanish artists, José del Pozo of Sevilla and José Guío of Madrid, but the latter had limited himself to scientific drawings and fallen victim to poor health; the former was lazy and was dismissed in Peru where he opened

Chief Tlupananul, Maquinna's main rival, drawn by Suría.

an art studio. Cardero, known as Little Pepe, showed increasing skill, but Malaspina wrote ahead to the Viceroyalty in Mexico City, requesting assistance while he awaited two more artists to be sent from Spain. Malaspina ended up taking aboard the Mexican engraver Tomás de Suría as a temporary measure.

The journal kept by de Suría was the only private diary of the voyage. De Suría was not allowed access to authorized accounts to check his facts, but his reportage provides a candid counterpoint to the reportage of Malaspina who was writing for posterity.

De Suría described his first day at Nootka: "The first thing they asked for was shells with the word 'pachitle conchi,' alternating this with saying 'Hispania Nutka' and then words which meant alliance and friendship. We were astonished to hear out of their mouths Latin words such as Hispania, but we concluded that perhaps they had learned this word in their trading with Englishmen...."

Later that afternoon de Suría was greeted by some Spanish sailors in a longboat. These were soldiers who had already arrived on the frigate *Concepción* from San Blas, commanded by Don Pedro Alberní, the man after whom the Vancouver Island town of Port Alberni is named. After his service in Nootka Sound with the Catalonian Volunteers in New Spain, Alberni became interim governor of California, where he died in 1803.

The original de Suría journal is kept at Yale University Library. An English translation was undertaken by Henry Raup Wagner in 1936 for the *Pacific Historical Review*. This version, in turn, was translated back into Spanish by Justino Fernández for a short book that added biographical details in 1939. This work was followed by a Master's thesis on de Suría by Agueda Jiménez Palayo of Guadalajara in 1972, under the direction of Donald C. Cutter.

De Suría was born in Valencia, Spain in April of 1761. He studied at the Royal Art Academy of San Fernando and accompanied his teacher Jerónimo Antonio Gil to Mexico at age seventeen. He married in 1788 and lived in Mexico City where he worked in the mint of the engraving office. With his wife's approval, he volunteered to join the Malaspina expedition and successfully negotiated the maintenance of his salary, travel expenses, suitable lodgings and continuance of his seniority when he returned to work. De Suría joined Malaspina on the *Descubierta* on March 27, 1791, at age thirty. Upon the expedition's return to Acapulco from Alaska and British Columbia, de Suría was given another eight months to prepare his drawings. These were forwarded to Spain.

Although de Suría's work gained the approval of Malaspina, his rewards were minimal. He remained in his former job as an engraver until his superior Gil died in 1798, whereupon de Suría held the position of chief engraver until 1806. He produced some religious art in his later years and died in 1844.

BOOKS: *Tomás de Surís' Quaderno que contiene el Ramo de Historia Natural y diario de la Expedicion del circulo de Globo...1791* (unpublished); Justino Fernández, *Tomás de Suría y su viaje con Malaspina, 1791* (Mexico City: Editorial Porrúa, 1939); *Journal of Tomás de Suría of His Voyage with Malaspina to the Northwest Coast of America in 1791,* ed. Donald C. Cutter (Fairfield, Washington: Ye Galleon, 1980); *Tomás de Suría: a l'expedició Malaspina–Alaska 1791* (Valencia: Generalitat Valenciana, 1995).

José Cardero's drawing of the Sutil *and* Mexicana.

DIONISIO ALCALÁ GALIANO

In the summer of 1792, Dionisio Alcalá Galiano in the *Sutil* completed the first circumnavigation of Vancouver Island accompanied by Cayetano Valdés y de Flores in the *Mexicana*.

Galiano and Valdés were detached from Malaspina's expedition to search for the Northwest Passage after Francisco Antonio Mourelle fell ill and was unable to take commmand of a voyage to the Strait of Juan de Fuca already planned by Viceroy Revilla Gigedo. An experienced hydrographer, Galiano spent two weeks working amicably in association with Valdés and Captain George Vancouver after the two Spanish commanders met the English captain off Point Grey near "Spanish Banks" and traded information on June 27, 1792. Although George Vancouver is right-

Dionisio Alcalá Galiano

fully known as the foremost cartographer of the B.C. coast, Galiano also produced excellent maps that were utilized by Vancouver in order to complete the mapping of the northwest coast. Galiano's account of his 1792 explorations was published ten years later in 1802 by the normally secretive Spanish government as a counterpoint to the 1798 publication of George Vancouver's extensive and precise charts. For many years a plaque at Spanish Banks marked their cooperative spirit. This plaque contained the words, "It was Dawn for Britain, but Twilight for Spain" until the phrase was expunged in March of 1984 in preparation for the visit of the King of Spain.

Cayetano Valdés

Born in Seville, Spain, on September 28, 1767, Valdés returned to Spain in 1793, commanded warships, was injured in the Battle of Trafalgar, was imprisoned and exiled for his liberal views, and died in Cádiz, Spain on February 6, 1835. Alcalá Galiano died on October 21, 1805 as the commander of the *Bahama* during the Battle of Trafalgar. Galiano Island is named for him, as well as a nature preserve on the north end of the island called Dionisio Park.

BOOKS: Dionisio Alcalá Galiano, *Relación del Viage hecho por las goletas Sutil y Mexicana en el año de 1792 para Reconocer el Estrecho de Fuca* (Madrid, 1802); *The Voyage of the Sutil and Mexicana 1792: The Last Spanish Exploration of the Northwest Coast of America,* ed. John Kendrick (Clark Co., 1991).

MANUEL QUIMPER

Accompanied by experienced pilots López de Haro and Juan Carrasco, Manuel Quimper was accorded two months to survey the largely uncharted northern and southern shores of the Strait of Juan de Fuca. He did so in the British fur-trading ship *Princess Royal*, confiscated by the Spanish in 1789 and renamed *Princesa Real*. His charts and his report of Haro Strait, now in the Archivo Historico Nacional in Madrid, encouraged the Spanish to make further explorations. While anchored in Puerto Quimper (Dungeness Bay) in Washington State, he became the first European to see Mount Baker.

Upon leaving Nootka Sound on May 31, 1790, Quimper went to Opitsat where he encouraged Chief Maquinna to make a return to Nootka. He also charted Clayoquot Sound. According to Grant Keddie in his excellent study *Songhees Pictorial* (Royal B.C. Museum, 2003), Quimper anchored outside Sooke Inlet, which he called Puerta de Revillagigedo, on June 18, 1790. He traded copper for sea otter skins, recorded the harvesting and trading of camas bulbs and witnessed three canoe burials. Here Quimper observed approximately 500 Indians who dressed somewhat differently from Indians on the western edge of Vancouver Island. Their cloaks included "the hair of sea otters and seals, and gull and duck feathers. Their hats are not of pyramidal form…but like those the Chinese wear in Macao."

Quimper also reached Puerto de San Juan (San Juan Bay) and Rada de Valdés y Bazan (Royal Roads), then crossed Juan de Fuca Strait to the San Juan Islands where he mapped two Dungeness villages and claimed them for Spain on July 4, 1790. He named his anchorage Bahía de Quimper (New Dungeness Bay) on July 8, and he charted Port Discovery and Neah Bay. Quimper set sail

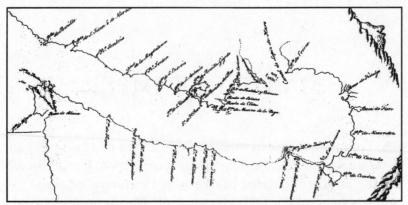

In 1790, Manuel Quimper's pilot Gonzalo López de Haro mistakenly drew Juan de Fuca Strait as a closed basin at its east end. George Vancouver proved otherwise.

for Nootka Sound on July 18, discovering Puerto de Cordova (Esquimault Harbour).

He claimed the present-day Victoria area for Spain in July of 1790. He proceeded south again to the Olympic Peninsula where he anchored in Freshwater Bay near the Elwha River on July 21, 1790. In his journal Quimper described being met by Indians in two canoes who directed the Spanish to fresh water and gave them salmonberries.

Quimper "christened" Mount Baker in Washington State, naming it "La Gran Montagna Carmelita" because it reminded him of the flowing white robes of the Carmelites. The peak would soon be renamed by Captain George Vancouver in 1792 after Lieutenant Joseph Baker who was the first to spot the snow-capped mountain from the *Discovery*.

In early August Quimper returned to Nootka but was unable to enter the harbour for six days due to fog. He returned to Monterey on September 1. Joined by Fidalgo in the *San Carlos*, they reached San Blas on November 13, 1790. Dates of Quimper's birth and death are unknown. His chart is kept in the Archivo Historico Nacional in Madrid.

BOOKS: *Spanish Explorations in the Strait of Juan de Fuca*, ed. Henry R. Wagner (Santa Ana, California, 1933).

JACINTO CAAMAÑO

O ne of the least-known Spanish explorers of the B.C. coast, but one of the most high-born, Jacinto Caamaño and his crew raised the first cross on the Queen Charlotte Islands, on Graham Island, on July 22, 1792.

During his expedition Caamaño wrote detailed accounts of his encounters with the Haida and Tsimshian. An incomplete English translation of Caamaño's 70-page journal was undertaken in 1938, but his chart and original manuscript, in the archives of the Ministerio de Asuntos Exteriores in Madrid, have not been widely consulted by English historians. Caamaño had previously commanded a 205-ton frigate built in the Philippines in 1780, *Our Lady of the Thornbush,* named after a Basque shrine to the Virgin Mary.

Prior to Captain Bodega y Quadra's planned meeting with Captain George Vancouver, when the Spanish needed to be certain there was not a Northwest Passage, Jacinto Caamaño was sent to re-explore Bucareli Bay and Douglas Channel in July of 1792. After considerable difficulties with weather and the Tsimshian, he concluded that the Fonte Strait connection with Hudson Bay did not exist. The Spanish had been misled by a chart made by the English fur trader Captain James Colnett.

Caamaño returned to Nootka Sound and reported this news to Captain Bodega y Quadra, thereby helping to facilitate a compromise settlement with the British and avoid an international conflict.

At Nootka in 1792, Caamaño dined with Captain George Vancouver and provided him with a copy of his charts. For this reason many of the place names devised by Caamaño have been retained.

Built in 1789, the battery of San Miguel still controlled the entrance to Nootka Sound when Jacinto Caamaño arrived in 1792.

Upon his return to Spain, Caamaño was knighted within Spain's oldest order of chivalry, the Military Order of Calatrava. He briefly served as military commander at San Blas, married in 1800, had eight children, and at age fifty became port captain of Guayaquil, Ecuador, in 1809.

Jacinto Caamaño died at Guayaquil in the 1830s. Caamaño's grandson became president of Ecuador in the 1880s.

A relic of Caamaño's expedition, a Spanish olive jar, was found off the east coast of Langara Island by two fishermen from Masset in 1985. Having consulted Caamaño's charts in Madrid, Maritime historian John Crosse has concluded this jar, manufactured between 1720 and 1790, could only have been left by the Caamaño expedition. "The only other Spanish vessel that had been in the area was the *Santiago* in 1774," he wrote, "but it had not sailed down the east side of Langara Island."

BOOKS: *Colecciones de Diarios y Relaciones para la Historia de los Viajes y Descubrimientos, VII: Comprende los viajes de Arteaga en 1792 y de Caamaño en 1792, por la costa NO. de América, Consejo Superior de Investigaciones Ceintíficas, Instituto Historico de Marina, 1975* [UBC Special Collections]; *The Journal of Don Jacinto Caamaño*, eds. Henry R. Wagner & W.A. Newcombe (*British Columbia Historical Quarterly* 2.3:189-222 & 2.4:265-301, 1938).

JOSÉ ESPINOSA Y TELLO

Lieutenant José Espinosa was picked up by the Malaspina expedition from Acapulco, along with Ciriaco Cevallos, an astronomer, because, among his various skills, Espinosa had been trained to operate two small Arnold chronometers from London that he brought on board to calculate longitude.

At Nootka Sound, Espinosa and Cevallos were sent by Malaspina to explore the inner channels of Muchalat Arm and Tlupana Arm, ultimately reaching Maquinna's winter village at the head of Tahsis Inlet. The Spaniards noted that Maquinna had an armoury of 14 muskets and that American John Kendrick had installed four windows in Maquinna's longhouse.

They were introduced to Maquinna's favourite wife, a sister of Chief Natzape, who was about age twenty and "whose attractive figure did not surprise us any less than the sentinel and the muskets.... If after a lengthy voyage one could judge beauty with accuracy," wrote Espinosa, "we would dare say that this vivacious girl exceeds in beauty the heroines of the novel, as they are pictured to us by the magic of poetry...." The Spaniards gave presents to all four of Maquinna's wives, visited other houses and guessed the overall population of the Mowachaht under Maquinna was 4,000. (Until disease and warfare decimated their numbers, there were approximately 28,000 Nuu-chah-nulth in the late 18th century on Vancouver Island. By the late 1990s their numbers had risen to approximately 6,000 from a low of 2,000 in the 1930s.)

BOOKS: *Memorias sobre las observaciones astronómicas hechas por los españoles en distintos lugares del globo, los cuales han servido de fundamento para las cartas de marear publicadas por la Dirección de los Trabajos Hidrográficos de Madrid* (Madrid: Imprenta Real, 1809).

L'Astrolabe *was one of two ships under Jean-François de la Pérouse who was enlisted to conduct a round-the-world scientific voyage to rival that of Captain James Cook.*

III
FRENCH

Jean-François de La Pérouse
Etienne Marchand
François Péron

JEAN-FRANÇOIS DE LA PÉROUSE

"The eye wandered with pain over masses of snow." —LA PÉROUSE

"The fame of Admiral Jean-François Galaup, Comte de La Pérouse has been unduly eclipsed by that of Captain James Cook."
—TRANSLATOR JULIUS S. GASSNER

The first Frenchman to see British Columbia was Jean-François de Galaup, Comte de La Pérouse. He is responsible for the first French book that contains eyewitness reports of B.C., although he never made landfall.

Born on August 23, 1741, near Albi, France, he entered the navy at age fifteen and fought the British off the coast of North America in the Seven Years' War. He gained prestige after two successful raids on English trading posts in Hudson Bay in 1782. Despite the disapproval of his family, he married a Creole named Louise-Eléonore Broudou from present-day Mauritius. La Pérouse was a great admirer of James Cook, and he was well-liked by his crew.

Eager for France to find a Northwest Passage, Louis XVI sent Jean-François de La Pérouse with 114 men and two vessels, *La Boussole* and *L'Astrolabe* (commanded by Captain de Langle), to explore the Pacific Northwest by sailing from Brest via Cape Horn, Easter Island and Hawaii. Given that his expedition was ostensibly scientific, La Pérouse was able to send dispatches back to Paris via the Spanish. He prophetically wrote, "Though the Russians are established in the north and the Spaniards to the south, many centuries will unquestionably elapse before these two nations meet; and there will long remain between them intermediary points, which might be occupied by other nations."

The French sighted Mount St. Elias at 59º north on June 23, 1786. La Pérouse wrote, "This sight of land, after a long voyage, usually excited feelings of delight; but on us it had not this effect. The eye wandered with pain over masses of snow, covering a barren soil, unembellished by a single tree." They reached Yakutat in Alaska on June 24 and traded with the Tlingit. La Pérouse was disgusted by the huge lip-pieces worn by the women and noted the Tlingit were passionately fond of gambling. "This is the grand source of their quarrels; and I do not hesitate to pronounce that this tribe would be completely exterminated if the use of any intoxicating liquor were added to these destructive vices."

Jean-François de La Pérouse

He sailed south, sighting the Queen Charlotte Islands and naming Sartine Island, now an ecological reserve northwest of Cape Scott, after French Minister of the Navy, Gabriel de Sartine, Count of Albi (1729–1801). Unable to enter Nootka Sound on August 25, La Pérouse never went ashore in British Columbia but his voyage was significant for spurring the English and Spanish to attempt an agreement for exploration and commercial control.

The French proceeded as far south as Monterey, California, before departing for Macao on September 24, 1786. They explored the Pacific for two more years, selling furs in the Orient. In December of 1787, the expedition lost 11 crew members and de Langle, commander of the *Astrolobe*, when they were murdered by Samoan Islanders.

Both ships, and all their men, were lost during a violent storm off Vanikoro Island in the Solomon Islands in 1788 or 1789. It was not until 1826 that an English captain, Peter Dillon, found evidence of the tragedy and later located the site of the sinkings. A French scholar who sailed with La Pérouse, M. de Lamanon, wrote, "...what will always distinguish this voyage, what will render the French nation truly glorious in the eyes of all philosophers, of our contemporaries and of posterity, will be our having frequented nations, reputed barbarous, without shedding a drop of blood." Journals from the La Pérouse expedition were sent back to France via Siberia in 1787 and via Botany Bay in 1788.

BOOKS: In 1797 the French government issued an elaborate report, with an atlas, entitled V*oyage de La Pérouse, Autour du Monde.* This formed the basis for *A Voyage Round The World, Performed in the Years 1786, 1787 and 1788* (London, 1798); *Voyages and Adventures of La Pérouse* (University of Hawaii Press, 1969).

ETIENNE MARCHAND

Next to La Pérouse, the most important 18th-century French explorer to reach the Pacific Northwest was Etienne Marchand, a merchant seaman who completed the second French circumnavigation of the globe. He was the first Frenchman to make a commercial voyage to British Columbia, and he provided some of the first detailed descriptions of heraldic carvings among the Haida. (Louis Antoine Bougainville completed the first French circumnavigation in 1769.)

Marchand was born in the West Indies, in Grenada, in 1755. He became intrigued with the Pacific Northwest after meeting the fur trader Nathanial Portlock on the island of St. Helena in 1789. Portlock apprised him of the profits to be made from sea otter pelts. Upon his return to France, Marchand had the 300-ton *Solide* built in Marseilles. He set sail in December of 1790, accompanied by a surgeon named Claude Roblet who also kept a journal of their 20-month voyage. The Marchand expedition traded with the Tlingit for 100 pelts when they were anchored near present-day Sitka, Alaska, but left after seeing signs of small-pox. Upon reaching the northern end of the Queen Charlotte Islands, Marchand's men made extensive forays along the shore-lines of various islands. The *Solide* reached Vancouver Island on August 4, 1791, where Marchand traded at Barkley Sound for three days, then sailed for Hawaii on September 8, 1791. The *Solide* was sighted by Robert Gray on the *Columbia* but Marchand and Gray did not make any contact.

After a brief stopover in Hawaii, Marchand crossed the Pacific to Macao only to discover the Chinese mandarins were not buying any furs. He met the ailing trader Joseph Ingraham who was "in the same boat." The physician Roblet tended to Ingraham. Still laden with furs, Marchand reluctantly sailed to Mauritius (then called the Ile de France), arriving on January 30, 1792. After an 11-week stopover, he sailed home by the Atlantic, arriving in Toulon harbour on August 14, 1792. Having lost only one man, due to a stroke, Marchand's expedition was an unusually safe one, but he had returned with his furs. His merchandising company sent the furs to Lyons where they were impounded by the Revolutionary government and eventually went rotten. Marchand later sailed on the *Sans-Souci* and died on Reunion Island (Ile de Bourbon), east of Madagascar, on May 15, 1793.

The greatest accomplishment of Marchand's travels turned out to be the posthumous, four-volume publication of his journals, edited by Charles Pierre Claret de Fleurieu. They include diaries by second-in-command Chanal and the surgeon Roblet, which contain observations of Tlingit and Haida villages.

Visiting a Haida village on Langara Island, Marchand provided the following description of an ornate house and its entrance way. "This opening is made in the thickness of a large trunk of a tree which rises perpendicularly in the middle of one of the fronts of the habitation, and occupies the whole of its height; it imi-tates the form of a gaping human mouth, or rather that of a beast, and it is surmounted by a hooked nose, about two feet in length, proportional in point of size, to the monstrous face to which it belongs....

"Over the door is seen the figure of a man carved in the attitude of a child in the womb, and remarkable for the extreme smallness of the parts which characterize his sex; and above this figure rises a gigantic statue of a man erect, which terminates the sculpture and the decoration of the portal; the head of this statue is dressed with a cap in the form of a sugar loaf, the height of which is almost equal to that of the figure itself. On the parts of the surface which are not occupied by the capital subjects, are interspersed carved figures of frogs or toads, lizards and other animals, the arms, legs, thighs and other parts of the human body...." The totems Marchand saw were decorated with bright red, black and apple-green colours. Similar artistry was absent from the houses on Graham Island.

BOOKS: Charles Pierre Claret de Fleurieu, *Voyage Autour du Monde, Pendant Les Années 1790, 1791, et 1792 par Etienne Marchand, précédé d'une Introduction Historique: Auquel on a Joint des Recherches sur les Terres Australes de Drake, et un Examen Critique du Voyage de Roggeween*, 4 vols. (Paris, 1798–1800); *Voyage Round the World, Performed During the Years 1790–92*, 2 vols. (London, 1801).

FRANÇOIS PÉRON

Just as the great Spanish scientist Moziño was unheralded in his lifetime—and for centuries afterwards—the work of the great French zoologist François Péron was mired in obscurity for more than a century. The Northwest Coast historian H.R. Wagner questioned his existence.

Known as the first trained zoologist to visit Australia, Péron is seldom recognized for his brief visit to Nootka Sound in June of 1796. Péron essentially hitched a ride from Sydney, as of February 18, 1796, aboard the *Otter*, an American trading vessel that

François Péron, drawn by the zoologist's friend Charles Alexandre Lambert Lesueur.

had embarked for Australia from Boston on August 20, 1795. Owned by Dorr and Sons, it was commanded by Ebenezer Dorr, formerly second mate of the *Hope* and later the *Fairy*. Arriving on Vancouver Island after a four-month Pacific crossing, Péron wrote, "At midday on the 21st, we arrived at an opening in the rocks, through which we could see a spacious bay dotted with many islands, large and small; this is the bay the English call Nootka Sound. As we entered the bay we sighted a ship in the anchorage at the western end of a string of ragged, and dangerous rocks. This was the Spanish schooner, *Sutil*, of San Blas, north of the isthmus of Panama. The commander of this ship, Captain Cuba, sent one of his officers to guide us into the harbor, which he called Friendly Bay. This officer informed us that as a result of protracted negotiations between England and Spain, the latter power had undertaken to abandon its claim to this port, and that the object of the *Sutil's* mission was to make a report on whether the English had done likewise, as agreed. The Spanish crown had reason to be distrustful, he said, as two English warships had been sighted in the vicinity. The object of our visit to Nootka was to procure fresh supplies, and in this we were cruelly disappointed. Captain Cuba showed us every mark of kindness, but he could not come to our aid."

The *Otter* traded on the coast for six months, made a stop in Hawaii on January 1, 1797, and reached Macao on February 13, 1797. By the time Péron finally returned to France—where he had been born in Cerilly on August 22, 1775, the son of a harness maker—he was primed to continue his remarkable life of adventure. Already he had joined the revolutionary army in 1792. He was taken prisoner and lost an eye before he could return home in 1794. This time he was determined to join the Baudin expedition to Terra Australis as part of a team of 22 civilian scientists on *Le Géographe* and *Le Naturaliste* that embarked in 1800. The deep antipathy that arose between Péron and Baudin is documented in their memoirs. Many of the scientists were forced to leave the two ships in Mauritius due to illness, so junior members such as Péron and his artist friend Charles Alexandre Lambert Lesueur rose to prominence.

With his medical training, Péron undertook studies in anatomy, anthropology, botany, zoology, meteorology, oceanography and naval hygiene. The multi-skilled naturalist also taught Lesueur some botany and taxidermy and how to trap animals for his drawings. At King George Sound in Australia, Péron, as chief zoologist, collected more than 1000 species of seashells and starfish. Péron and Lesueur killed and preserved countless specimens in jars filled with alcohol, ultimately returning to France in 1804 with more than 100,000 specimens in 33 packing cases aboard *Le Naturaliste*.

In 1806, Emperor Napoleon gave his permission for Lesueur and Péron to prepare their findings in a *Voyage de découvertes aux Terres Australes*, to be written by Péron and illustrated by Lesueur. A first volume appeared in 1807 but Péron died of tuberculosis on December 14, 1810. Under the control of map maker Louis de Freychinet, a second volume appeared in 1816. Péron's opinionated memoirs appeared in 1824 but most of the natural history collections made by Péron and Lesueur were not exhibited. Lesueur had to wait until 1846 to regain access to his drawings and Péron's research. It took almost 200 years for their collections to be finally shown to the public.

BOOKS: *Memoires du Capitaine François Péron, Tomes I et II* (Paris: Brissot-Thivars, Libraire Bossange Frères, 1824); Colin Wallace, *The Lost Australia of François Péron* (London: Nottingham Court Press, 1983).

James Cook receives pride of place at Victoria's inner harbour, outside the Empress Hotel and the Parliament of British Columbia. He reached Nootka Sound in 1778.

I V
COOK & CREW

James Cook
John Rickman
Heinrich Zimmerman
William Ellis
John Ledyard
James King
James Burney
David Samwell
John Webber
William Bayly
James Trevenen
George Gilbert

JAMES COOK

Usually cited as the first European to set foot in British Columbia, James Cook posthumously published the fourth-earliest account in English of the first British landing in British Columbia.

No preceding voyage had surveyed so much territory as James Cook's third and final Pacific voyage that reached Nootka Sound on March 30, 1778. The great, dispassionate mariner navigated between 49º S in the Antarctic to 70º N in the Arctic, while amassing new information on the peoples, coastlines and islands of the five great oceans.

The lionization of James Cook has been questioned by Sri Lankan anthropologist Gananath Obeyeskere in *The Apotheosis of Captain Cook* in which he debunks the notion that Hawaiians presumed Cook was their god Lono returned to them. Obeyeskere alleges Cook was a narcissistic, melancholic bore who appeared enlightened at home but was increasingly tyrannical at sea, contemptuous of natives with their "savage ways," burning villages and flogging his men for misdemeanors.

Cook's much-edited journals became the main catalyst for the North Pacific fur trade as soon as his men learned that sea otter fur was highly prized by wealthy mandarins in China. Cook observed, "There is not the least doubt that a very beneficial fur trade might be carried on with the inhabitants of this vast coast."

The story goes that Cook was also responsible for the word Nootka. Having dropped anchor in Resolution Cove off Bligh Island, keeping his distance from Yuquot, Cook and his men watched the Mowachaht approach in their canoes, calling out, "Itchme nutka! Itchme nutka!" They were urging Cook to sail his two ships around Bligh Island to an anchorage nearer their village.

Cook assumed they were introducing themselves as the Nootka, or else providing the name of their settlement. Martínez, who became the Spanish fort commander, corroborated this story in a diary entry for September 30, 1789, when he wrote, "the name of Nootka, given to this port by the English, is derived from the poor understanding between them and the natives.... Captain Cook's men, asking [the Indians] by signs what the port was called, made for them a sign in their hand, forming a circle and then dissolving it, to which the natives responded Nutka, which means 'to give way' [retroceder]. Cook named it in his diary 'entrada del Rey Jorge o de Nutka,' and the rest of the ships have known it by the latter, which is Nutka, for which reason they have forced the Indians also to know it by that name; nevertheless, at first the new name always seemed strange; the true name by the natives is Yuquot, which means 'for this.'" Belgian missionary Father A.J. Brabant later deduced noot-ka-eh is a verb meaning "go round."

Conversely, Cook was not responsible for the term Friendly Cove. That name for Maquinna's summer village at Yuquot arose from the visit of the English fur trader James Strange in 1786. Although Cook took care to anchor away from Yuquot, his crewmen did variously record their contacts with Chief Maquinna's people and have since been blamed for the introduction of venereal disease.

After continuing north through the Bering Strait and into the Arctic Ocean, Cook found great walls of ice blocked his search for a Northwest Passage. Cook headed back to the warmer Sandwich Islands (Hawaii) where he was famously stabbed to death on February 14, 1779. He had been investigating the alleged theft of a large boat by an islander. In frustration, Cook captured the Hawaiian king at Kealakekua Bay, hoping to ransom him for the return of his boat. Sensing danger, Cook released the king before a crowd of several thousand islanders. When an islander made a threatening gesture, Cook turned and fired. The extent to which Cook provoked his own demise is a matter of conjecture. The crowd rushed forward. During the fracas, Cook was stabbed and drowned in the surf. Four shipmates were also killed as his men fled back to their ship. It has never been clear whether Cook was stabbed in the back or not.

Lieutenant James King did not witness the killing but he reported "it was remarked that while he faced the natives, none of them had offered him any violence, but that having turned about, to give his orders to the boats, he was stabbed in the back, and fell with his face into the water." There has been speculation that Cook was ill at the time, and perhaps his judgment of the situation was impaired. Evidence that he had become unusually cruel towards his crew is contained in John Ledyard's memoir of the voyage. The Sandwich Islanders hacked Cook's body into sections, taking it away. When some of Cook's body parts and his scalp were returned a few days later, Cook's crew went on a rampage, shooting many islanders and burning their village. A week later, the remains of Captain James Cook were buried at sea.

The British Admiralty published an edited account of Cook's voyages in three quarto volumes and a large atlas in 1784–1785, now generally known as *A Voyage to the Pacific Ocean*. The journals were heavily edited by Dr. John Douglas, Bishop of Salisbury. As commissioned by the Lords of the Admiralty, Douglas embellished much of Cook's original journals with material gleaned from Cook's officers. In particular, Douglas extrapolated from Cook's reports of ritualistic dismemberment among the Nootka, beginning the belief that the Indians engaged in cannibalism when Cook had, in fact, described them as "docile, courteous, good-natured people." Some of the more sensational revelations added to the text were designed to encourage the spreading of "the blessings of civilization" among the heathens and to help sell books.

For almost 200 years Douglas' version of Cook's writings was erroneously accepted as Cook's own. Cook's journal, with its bloody ending supplied by James King, proved popular. Within three days of its publication in 1784, the first printing was sold out. There were five additional printings that year, plus 14 more by the turn of the century. Translations were made throughout

Europe. The original version of Cook's journal was edited by J.C. Beaglehole and finally published for scholars in the 1960s. It reveals that Cook was a somewhat dull reporter, more interested in geography than anthropology.

The profits from the publication of Cook's journals went to the estates of Cook, James King and Charles Clerke (Commander of the *Discovery*), with a one-eighth share for William Bligh, master of the *Resolution*, because his surveying work was so essential. The irascible Bligh wrote in ink on the title page of his own copy, "None of the Maps and Charts in this publication are from the original drawings of Lieut. Henry Roberts, he did no more than copy the original ones from Captain Cook who besides myself was the only person that surveyed and

James Cook's undoctored journal about the Pacific Northwest was not published until 1967.

laid the Coast down, in the *Resolution*. Every Plan & Chart from C. Cook's death are exact copies of my works."

The major English voyages to British Columbia in Cook's wake were commanded by Hanna (1785 and 1786); Strange (1786); Lowrie and Guise (1786–1787); Meares and Tipping (1786–1787); Portlock and Dixon (1786–1787); Duncan and Colnett (1787–1788); Barkley (1787), Meares and Douglas (1788); Douglas and Funter (1789); and Colnett and Hudson (1789).

Information about the life and times of James Cook is easily gleaned from dozens of biographies (see appendix) and www.captaincooksociety.com.

JOHN RICKMAN

"King exaggerates the influence of what Lieutenant Rickman did at the southern point of Kealakekua Bay, and blames the 'fatal turn in the affair' on Rickman." —HISTORIAN GAVIN KENNEDY

A s mentioned in the introduction, the English Admiralty required all copies of diaries kept at sea to be relinquished at the end of exploratory and scientific voyages. Cook's third voyage ended in October of 1780. Thus when John Rickman published his account in 1781, it was the first eyewitness account of British Columbia written and published in English—and he had to do so anonymously. Rickman was a little-known Second Lieutenant aboard the *Discovery* when Captain James Cook visited Nootka. His version of events went through three printings in 1781. Reprinted in Philadelphia in 1783, it was revised in England in 1785. Editions also appeared in German and French.

It was Rickman who first conveyed to the public the chilling details of Captain Cook's death and dismemberment in Hawaii. Possibly Rickman took the risk of publication because he correctly anticipated Lieutenant James King would insinuate in the official version of the voyage that Rickman's conduct had been partially responsible for the assault on Cook.

During the beach melée on February 14, 1779, Rickman had led a party that killed one of the chiefs, Kareemoo, about a mile from the confrontation with Cook. "Muskets were fir'd by Mr Rickmans party," wrote James King, "who were in boats at the Soermost part of the bay, keeping in the Canoes, in doing so they killd a Very principal Chief."

Derivative works by Andrew Kippis and Reverend William Ellis supported King's view that Rickmen's men had precipitated the crisis. Much later Reverend Ellis wrote, "… a man came running from the other side of the bay, entered the crowd almost breathless, and exclaimed, 'It is war!—the foreigners have commenced hostilities, have fired on a canoe from one of their boats, and killed a chief.' This enraged some of our people, and alarmed the chiefs, as they feared Captain Cook would kill the king. The people armed themselves with stones, clubs and spears. All the chiefs did the same."

William Bligh strongly implied that Rickman was not at all blameworthy. The accounts of James Burney, David Samwell and Thomas Edgar corroborated this opinion. "Cook's orders and actions made a confrontation inevitable," concluded historian Gavin Kennedy in *The Death of Captain Cook.* The marine guard accompanying Cook fired in a panic and fled, leaving Cook to the mercies of the mob. It is likely that King and Ellis, among others, agreed to scapegoat Rickman as a means of protecting Cook's reputation.

Less encumbered by the politics within the British Admiralty, Ledyard, the American, offered some of the more astute and independent reportage. He took the radical view that Cook was himself chiefly to blame—not the Hawaiians, nor Rickman.

When the supremely confident captain was alerted that Kareemoo's brother vowed revenge, "Cook attended to what the man said, and desired him to shew him the Indian that had dared to attempt a combat with him, and as soon as he was pointed out Cook fired at him with a blank. The Indian perceiving he received no damage from the fire rushed from without the crowd a second time, and threatened any one that should appose [sic] him. Cook perceiving this fired a ball, which entering the Indian's groin he fell and was drawn off by the rest."

For many years it was presumed that the author of John Rickman's anonymously published memoir was John Ledyard because Ledyard had used Rickman's memoir as a basis for his own factual information. The prolific British Columbian historian Frederic Howay clarified the matter in 1921 with his contribution to the *Washington Historical Quarterly* called "Authorship

John Rickman's book was the first account written and published in English to describe British Columbia. This depiction of the murder of Captain James Cook in Hawaii served as the frontispiece for Rickman's journal. It is a detail from a larger painting by Francis Jukes, after a picture by John Clevely. He, in turn, based his painting on a drawing by his brother, James Clevely, a carpenter on the *Resolution*.

of Anonymous Account of Captain Cook's Last Voyage."

BOOKS: John Rickman, *Journal of Captain Cook's last voyage to the Pacific Ocean on Discovery; performed in the Years 1776, 1777, 1778, 1779, illustrated with Cuts, and a Chart, shewing the Tracts of the Ships employed in this Expedition. Faithfully Narrated from the original MS* (London: Printed for E. Newberry, at the corner of St. Paul's Church Yard, 1781); *An Authentic Narrative of a Voyage to the Pacific Ocean Performed by Captain Cook, and Captain Clerke, 2 vols.* (Philadelphia: Printed and sold by Robert Bell, in Third Street, 1783).

HEINRICH ZIMMERMAN

Heinrich Zimmerman, as coxswain on the *Discovery* for Cook's third voyage, surreptitiously kept a shorthand journal that appeared as *Reise um die Welt mit Capitain Cook* (Mannheim, 1781). This journal appeared three years before the official English version of Cook's *Voyages* was released and two years prior to John Ledyard's account.

Zimmerman was a German from the town of Speir in Holland (now Speyer in Germany). His descriptions of Hawaii sparked an interest in the islands, but he also offered some of the first descriptions of West Coast Indians. Zimmerman published the first record of the "Nootka" language, specifically transcribing the Nootka word for iron—*tsikimin,* or *sickeminnee, sickemaillé* and *sick-a-minny.* For the "big nail" he wrote *tschikimli.*

According to Howay's translation of Zimmerman's journal, he described the Mowachaht as being "skilful in the use of their crossbows and in general are a very warlike and stout-hearted people, and as far as we could discover, in a constant state of warfare amongst themselves, the slain being devoured." He claimed they dried human flesh "which they ate with relish and which they wished us to try."

The likes of Zimmerman and Ledyard understood there was an avid audience for New World accounts of cannibalism. In Germany, Hans Staden's *The True History and Description of a Country of Savages, A Naked and Terrible People, Eaters of Men's Flesh, Who Dwell in the New World Called America* (1557) had been a bestseller. Staden, from Homberg in Hessen, had embarked on the first of his voyages to Brazil at age twenty. Shipwrecked, he washed ashore at Itanhaem, commanded a small fort for the Portuguese, and was captured by the Tupinamba Indians who allegedly ate their

Heinrich Zimmermanns

von

Wißloch in der Pfalz,

Reise um die Welt,

mit

Capitain Cook.

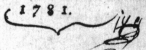

Mannheim

bei C. F. Schwan, kuhrfürstl. Hofbuchhändler,

1781.

Zimmermann's book alerted Europe to the existence of the Pacific Northwest.

prisoners to "incorporate" their good qualities. Staden survived by his wits for eight months, then escaped on a French ship. His detailed and well-illustrated memoir has been through 80 editions and is considered a classic document of Brazilian history. Zimmerman's 100-page book was soon suppressed in Germany, at the request of the British Admiralty. A French edition appeared in 1782. A Dutch translation followed.

BOOKS: Heinrich Zimmerman, *Reise um die Welt, mit Capitain Cook* (Mannheim, 1781); *Zimmerman's Captain Cook, 1781,* edited by Frederic W. Howay (Toronto: Ryerson, 1930).

WILLIAM ELLIS

O ne of the most obscure but earliest documents to recall the Pacific Coast of British Columbia is a journal published by an assistant surgeon on the *Discovery* and later the *Resolution.* The first edition of William Ellis' diary appeared two years prior to the release of Cook's narrative. Needing money, Ellis contravened the dictates of the Admiralty and sold his narrative to a bookseller for 50 guineas.

The *Resolution* left Plymouth in July of 1776 and the *Discovery* set sail in August. They rounded the Cape of Good Hope on November 30, reaching Tasmania (Van Diemen's Land) and New Zealand before heading north to discover the Raratonga and Cook Islands. The crews rested for four months at Tahiti. Captains Cook and Clerke discovered and named the Hawaiian Islands as the Sandwich Islands, then proceeded to the B.C. and Alaska coasts.

William Ellis recalled the killing of Captain Cook upon their return to Hawaii, followed by Captain Clerke's stint as commander until he succumbed to tuberculosis shortly after embarkation from Petropavlovsk in Alaska. Captains King of the *Discovery* and Gore of the *Resolution* returned to Petropavlovsk, buried Clerke, and sailed back to England. Ellis' narrative was reprinted several times, although Ellis did not receive a share of the profits, having relinquished his copyright for a lump sum.

The National Library of Canada retains a copy of Ellis' two-volume *An Authentic Narrative of a Voyage Performed by Captain Cook and Captain Clerke* (London: Printed for G. Robinson, J. Sewell and J. Debrett, 1782).

BOOKS: *An Authentic Narrative of a Voyage Performed by Captain Cook and Captain Clerke, in his Majesty's Ships Resolution and Discovery, During the Years 1776, 1777, 1778, 1779 and 1780; In Search of a North-West Passage Between the Continents of Asia and America. Including a Faithful Account of all their Discoveries, and the Unfortunate Death of Captain Cook, Illustrated with a Chart and a Variety of Cuts* (London: G. Robinson, J. Sewell and J. Debrett, 1782; reprinted 1783, 1784).

JOHN LEDYARD

John Ledyard, the most travelled American of the 18th century, was described by Thomas Jefferson as "a man of genius, of some science, and of fearless courage and enterprise."

Even though Ledyard published some of the earliest impressions of British Columbia, he is little-known in Canada, perhaps because his roots are American and not British.

Ledyard was a Connecticut Yankee who began to earn the title "America's Marco Polo" at an early age. Born in Groton, Connecticut in 1751, he studied law and theology at Dartmouth in 1772, intending to become a missionary, but his family was poor, the result of his father's death at sea.

One of his classmates at Dartmouth was an Indian who taught him how to paddle a canoe. In 1773, Ledyard chopped down a white pine, carved a 50-foot-long canoe on the banks of the Connecticut River and set off with the Greek Testament and Ovid as his reading material. He paddled 140 miles to Hartford, then reached New York.

As a sailor he visited the Barbary Coast and the West Indies in late 1773, then enlisted as a corporal in the British Navy at Gibraltar in 1776. In Plymouth he signed on for duty with Captain Cook's third voyage that took him to the Canary Islands, Cape Verde Islands, Cape of Good Hope, Tasmania, New Zealand, Tahiti, California, Oregon, the Bering Sea, Unalaska Island, the eastern coast of Asia and the western coast of Vancouver Island. Ledyard described his momentous arrival at Nootka Sound with Captain Cook on March 30, 1778.

"We entered this inlet about 4 o'clock in the afternoon. The extremes of the opening at the entrance were about 2 miles distant, and we had the prospect of a snug harbour. It was a matter of doubt with many of us whether we should find any inhabitants here, but we had scarcely entered the inlet before we saw that hardy, that intrepid, that glorious creature man approaching us from the shore....

"Night approaching we came to an anchor between one of those islands and the eastern shore about one quarter of a mile from each. In the evening we were visited by several canoes full of the natives; they came abreast our ship within two rods of us and there staid the whole night, without offering to approach nearer or to withdraw farther from us, neither would they converse with us. At the approach of day they departed in the same reserve and silence. On the 30th we sent our boats to examine a small cove in the opposite island, which answering our wishes we moved with both ships into it and moored within a few rods of the surrounding beach."

Ledyard provided one of the first and best records of Mowachaht behaviour and attitudes in the 18th century.

"Water and wood they charged us nothing for. Capt. Cook would not credit this fact when he first heard it and went in person to be assured of it, and persisting in a more peremptory tone in his demands, one of the Indians took him by the arm and thrust him from him, pointing the way for him to go about his business. Cook was struck with astonishment, and turning to his people with a smile mixed with admiration exclaimed, 'This is an American indeed!' and instantly offered this brave man what he thought proper to take; after which the Indian took him and his men to his dwelling and offered them such as he had to eat."

Upon his return to England in 1780, Ledyard was forced to give his journals to the Admiralty.

Ledyard served in the British navy for two more years, reaching America at the close of the Revolution in December 1782. During a seven-day leave he visited his mother, brothers and sisters whom he had not seen for eight years. Unwilling to fight for the British against his American brethren, he deserted at Huntington.

Ledyard spent the first four months of 1783 at Thomas Seymour's home in Hartford. When friends persuaded Ledyard to recount his adventures with Cook, he was not averse to using portions of John Rickman's account to refresh his memory.

Ironically, Ledyard's book served as a landmark volume for copyright legislation in the United States. As a former student of the law, Ledyard successfully petitioned the Connecticut Assembly for the right of exclusive publication. Although the copyright designation did not appear in the volume, Ledyard's memoir became the first book to be issued in the United States under a copyright law of the sort that is now prevalent, to protect the rights of the author. Provisions of the Connecticut copyright law were soon copied by other states, leading to a national copyright law in 1790.

Ledyard's memoirs provide an uncensored eye-witness narrative of Cook's murder at Kealakekua Bay. Also killed were Royal Marine Corporal John Thomas, Privates Theophilus Hinks, John Allen and Tom Fatchett and many Hawaiians. Unlike most of his British contemporaries, Ledyard was clearly willing to consider the confrontation from the perspective of the Hawaiians. His account of the great hero's death was critical of Cook's arrogant attitude towards the Hawaiians and he alleges Cook was jealous of Vitus Bering.

Ledyard's memoirs constitute the first great travel literature by an American to be published in the United States. His publisher was Nathaniel Patten, a Hartford printer who dedicated the book to Governor Jonathan Trumbull, George Washington's "Brother Jonathan" of Revolutionary fame.

It soon became Ledyard's great ambition to become the first American to cross the continent on foot. Thomas Jefferson wrote of their meeting in Paris in 1786: "I suggested to him the enterprise of exploring the western part of our continent by passing through St. Petersburg to Kamtchatka and procuring a passage thence in some of the Russian vessels to Nootka Sound, whence he might make his way across the continent to the United States; and I undertook to have the permission of the empress of Russia solicited."

Ledyard devised a plan to travel across Russia and Siberia, then onto Alaska, then down to the Mississippi River. With two hunting dogs as companions, he set forth but failed to cross the Baltic ice from Stockholm to Abo. Reconsidering, he walked from Stockholm to St. Petersburg, arriving barefoot and penniless in 1787. Undeterred, Ledyard managed to accompany a Scottish physician named Brown to Siberia. Leaving Dr. Brown at Barnaul, he went on to Tomsk and Irkutsk, visited Lake Baikal, and descended the Lena to Yakutsk, but Catherine the Great sent orders for him to be arrested. At Irkutsk he was accused of being a French spy and banished from Russia. He was sent back to Poland.

In 1788, Ledyard speculated about possible racial connections between Asian and American aboriginals, providing grist for similar anthropological arguments that were advanced in the two centuries that followed.

Ledyard's wanderlust continued. Back in London, he signed on for duty with Sir Joseph Banks and the African Association for an overland expedition from Alexandria to the Niger. At age thirty-seven, John Ledyard died in Cairo on January 10, 1789, killed by an overdose of vitriolic acid.

Extracts from Ledyard's private correspondence with Thomas Jefferson and others are provided in Jared Sparks' *Life of John Ledyard*. Ledyard's comments about women give an indication of his seriousness and character.

"I have always remarked that women in all countries are civil and obliging, tender and humane; that they are ever inclined to be gay and cheerful, timorous and modest; and that they do not hesitate like men, to perform a generous action. Not haughty, not arrogant, not supercilious, they are full of courtesy, and fond of society; more liable in general to err than man, but in general also more virtuous, and performing more good actions, than he. To a woman, whether civilized or savage, I never addressed myself in the language of decency and friendship, without receiving a decent and friendly answer.

"With man it has often been otherwise. In wandering over the barren plains of inhospitable Denmark, through honest Sweden and frozen Lapland, rude and churlish Finland, unprincipled Russia, and the wide spread regions of the wandering Tartar; if hungry, dry, cold, wet, or sick, the women have ever been friendly to me, and uniformly so. And add to this virtue, so worthy the appellation of benevolence, their actions have been performed in so free and kind a manner, that if I was dry, I drank the sweetest draught, and if hungry, I eat the coarsest morsel with a double relish."

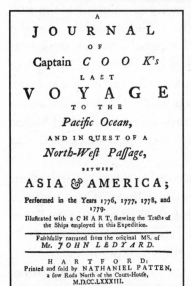

A

J O U R N A L

O F

Captain C O O K's

L A S T

V O Y A G E

T O T H E

Pacific Ocean,

AND IN QUEST OF A

North-West Passage,

BETWEEN

ASIA & AMERICA;

Performed in the Years 1776, 1777, 1778, and 1779.

Illustrated with a C H A R T, shewing the Tracts of the Ships employed in this Expedition.

Faithfully narrated from the original MS. of Mr. J O H N L E D Y A R D.

H A R T F O R D: Printed and fold by NATHANIEL PATTEN, a few Rods North of the Court-House, M.DCC.LXXXIII.

Title page of John Ledyard's book.

BOOKS: John Ledyard, *A Journal of Captain Cook's Last Voyage to the Pacific Ocean, and in Quest of a North-West Passage, between Asia & America; Performed in the Years 1776, 1777, 1778, and 1789* (Hartford, Connecticut: Nathaniel Patten, 1783).

JAMES KING

Lieutenant James King was among the crewmen from Captain Cook's third voyage who brought furs to Canton and discovered their immense trading value. When a merchant offered 300 Spanish dollars (or "pieces of eight") for 20 sea otter furs, plus some silks, King demanded 1,000 and settled for 800. Back in Macao he discovered one crewman had sold a single prime skin for 120 Spanish dollars and Midshipman James Trevenen had gained 300 Spanish dollars for a single fur which he had obtained at Nootka Sound in exchange for a broken belt buckle. William Bligh received £15 for six skins he had obtained at Prince William Sound in exchange for 12 beads. From these revelations arose the fur trade on the coast of British Columbia.

At Nootka Sound, King noted the importance of music within the culture of Maquinna's people. Describing their arrival at Nootka Sound, he observed, "The greatest number of the Canoes remained in a cluster around us til ten O'clock, & as they had no arms, & appeared very friendly, we did not care how long they staid to entertain themselves, & perhaps us: a man repeated a few words in tune, & regulated the meaning by beating against the Canoe sides, after which they all joined in a song, that was by no means unpleasant to the Ear.

"A young man with a remarkable soft effeminate voice afterward sung by himself, but he ended so suddenly & unexpectedly, which being accompanied by a peculiar gesture, made us all laugh, & he finding that we were not ill pleased repeated his song several times.

"As they were now very attentive & quiet in list'ning to their diversions, we judg'd they might like our musick, & we ordered the Fife & drum to play a tune; these were the only people we

James King

had seen that ever paid the smallest attention to those or any of
our musical Instruments, if we except the drum, & that only I
suppose from its noise & resemblance to their own drums; they
observed the profoundest silence, & we were sorry that the dark
hindered our seeing the effect of this musick on their counte-
nances. Not to be outdone in politeness they gave us another
song, & we then entertained them with French horns, to which
they were equally attentive, but gave us no more songs in return,
& soon after went away, excepting a few boats that kept paddling
around us all that night which was a very cold one."

James King was born in 1750 and died in 1784. He became the
subject of a biography by John Bolton King in 2004.

[James King contributed to the completion of James Cook's *Journal*.]

JAMES BURNEY

As first lieutenant on the *Discovery*, James (Jem) Burney made maps of Cook's approach to British Columbia and recorded the first entrance into Nootka Sound. Describing the first British contacts with B.C., he wrote, "...in the evening, several of the larger Canoes saluted us, by making a Circuit around the ships and giving 3 Halloos at their departure. They paddle in most excellent time, the foremost man every 3rd or 4th Stroke making flourishes with his paddle. The halloo is a single note in which they all join, swelling it out in the middle and letting the sound die away. In a Calm with the hills around us, it had an effect infinitely superior to what might be imagined from any thing so simple."

Burney first served under Cook with fifteen-year-old George Vancouver during Cook's second major voyage (1772–1775) to the South Seas. He was the brother of the English diarist and writer Fanny Burney who described Captain Cook as "the most moderate, humane, and gentle circumnavigator that ever went upon discoveries."

In his own journal James Burney verified Cook's failure to find the opening to the Strait of Juan de Fuca and provided a detailed account of Cook's final days. It was Burney who took command of the *Discovery* after Cook was killed in Hawaii. After a lengthy career at sea, he retired as a rear-admiral and published a five-volume work called *A Chronological History of the Discoveries in the South Seas or Pacific Ocean*. Copies of his original journal are in the British Museum and the Mitchell Library, Sydney.

BOOKS: G.E. Manwaring, *My Friend the Admiral, the Life, Letters, and Journals of Rear-Admiral James Burney, F.R.S.* (London: George Routledge & Sons, Ltd., 1931); *Journal of James Burney, 1778* (Canberra: National Library, 1975).

DAVID SAMWELL

As the first European physician in British Columbia, Welshman David Samwell understood that one of the worst perils of a seafaring life was venereal disease. Having served as a surgeon's mate on Captain Cook's third voyage, first on the *Resolution* and then on the *Discovery*, Samwell, a parson's son, included a reference to venereal diseases in the lengthy title of his memoir.

Samwell had observed and recorded the devastating effects of venereal disease brought to Hawaii by Cook's men. "They had a Clap, their Penis was much swell'd, & inflamed," concurred James King in dismay, when Cook's men returned to winter in Hawaii ten months after making their first visit. While Captain Cook was a firm disciplinarian who favoured many of the ideals of Quakerism, it remained an ongoing battle to curtail or limit sexual relations between his crewmen and the indigenous women of Tahiti, Hawaii and Vancouver Island.

As Cook himself commented in Hawaii, watching "hogs and women" coming offshore in canoes, "it was not possible to keep the latter out of the Ship and no women I ever met with were more ready to bestow their favours." In the preceding month Samwell recorded the nature of relations between Cook's crewmen and Hawaiian women. "When any one of us sees a handsome Girl in a Canoe that he has a mind to, upon waving his Hand to her she immediately jumps overboard & swims to the Ship, where we receive her in our arms like another Venus just rising from the Waves; both Men & Women come on board the ships in great Numbers and during the whole time of trafficking with them it is nothing but one Scene of Noise & Confusion on board the Ships & all round them."

A substantive investigation of the sex trade at Nootka Sound was undertaken by Eliot Fox-Povey and published in the Summer 2003 edition of *British Columbia Historical News*. "The organized sale of sex to Europeans seems to have come about through adaptation not imposition...," Fox-Povey claims. "When Europeans proposed a trade in sex with women, slavery provided Nuu-chah-nulth elites with a class of sex workers who were outside of Nuu-chah-nulth social rules of sexual modesty, and whose work would only re-affirm existing wealth relationships."

Samwell and Charles Clerke of the *Discovery* both recorded that sailors first scrubbed many of the women brought onto the ships prior to having sex. Samwell also observed of trading relations overall, "In general in their dealings with us they acted in a fair part tho' they made no scruple of stealing when the opportunity offered; but upon being detected they would immediately return whatever they had taken and laugh in our faces, as they considered it as a piece of Dexterity that did them credit rather than dishonor."

Samwell's journal was published after Captain Cook's journal became a runaway bestseller. "His great Qualities," Samwell wrote, "I admired beyond anything I can express—I gloried in him—and my Heart bleeds to this Day whenever I think of his Fate." Samwell's account of Captain Cook's murder is usually considered one of the more reliable of the several that were rendered. It was excerpted and widely circulated. The English author Andrew Kippis used it in his *Biographia Britannica* as well as his biography *The Life of Captain James Cook* (1788).

Back in Britain, Samwell wrote poetry and supported Welsh causes. He later grew nostalgic for his extraordinary adventures with Cook and once wrote, "It is an article of Faith with every one of us that there never was such a collection of fine Lads take us for all in all, got together as there was in the *Resolution & Discovery*." As a physician he treated British prisoners-of-war in Paris in

1798. That same year he returned to London where he died of drink and laudanum.

Although Samwell had limited success treating venereal disease, he took justifiable pride in helping Cook keep his crew free of scurvy. "We did not loose one Man by Sickness—a Circumstance unparallel'd in ye History of Navigation."

BOOKS: *A Narrative of the Death of Captain James Cook to which are Added Some Particulars, Concerning his Life and Character, and Observations Respecting the Introduction of the Venereal Disease into the Sandwich Islands* (London, 1786); reprinted within Sir Maurice Holmes' *Captain Cook and Hawaii: A Narrative by David Samwell* (San Francisco: David Magee; London: Francis Edwards, Ltd., 1957).

JOHN WEBBER

As the draughtsman on Cook's visit to Nootka, John Webber produced drawings that appeared in the Admiralty's official version of Cook's journal, greatly contributing to its popularity. As the second-most prolific artist on the voyage, he would render 326 paintings and portraits, including preliminary sketches, prior to his death in 1793. Until the advent of photography, Cook's third expedition was the most extensively documented voyage in history.

Webber painted Cook three times from life, twice in 1776 and once in 1777. The third portrait was painted in Tahiti and given by Cook to his friend Chief Tu (Otoo). It has since disappeared. The first two paintings are in the National Portrait Gallery, London, and the National Art Gallery, Wellington. John Webber's posthumous 1782 portrait of Cook is one of five known surviving portraits produced in the 18th century. A less severe representation than the better-known portrait by Nathaniel Dance, it was acquired in 2000 by the National Portrait Gallery in London.

John Webber's portrait of a woman at Nootka Sound, 1778.

John Webber's portrait of a man at Nootka Sound, 1778.

John Webber was born circa 1752 in London as the son of a Swiss sculptor. He apprenticed for three years with the Swiss landscape artist Johann Aberli, then studied in Paris. At age twenty-four he was admitted to study at the Royal Academy in London where he exhibited for the first time in 1776. He was recommended to serve as the official artist on the *Resolution* by the Swiss naturalist Daniel Solander who had sailed with Cook on his first voyage to the South Seas. Webber joined Cook's crew at Plymouth and later produced several noteworthy images of Nootka Sound.

Fifteen years after Webber's death in 1793, some of his pictures were reproduced as aquatints in a book.

BOOKS: *Views in the South Seas, from drawings by the late James Webber, Draftsman on board the Resolution, Captain James Cooke* [sic], *from the year 1776 to 1780* (London, 1808).

WILLIAM BAYLY

Born in 1737, the self-taught astronomer and mathematician William Bayly had served as an assistant in the Royal Observatory prior to sailing as an astronomer for Cook's second and third voyages. His work is incorporated into King's version of Cook's final voyage. He later edited his own calculations for a book. One of Malaspina's two Spanish astronomers, José Espinosa y Tello, likewise published *Memorias sobre las observaciones astronómicas hechas por los navegantes españoles en distintos lugares del globo* in 1809. Bayly was Headmaster of the Royal Navy Academy at Portsmouth from 1785 to 1807. He died in 1810. Several of his charts are displayed at the Vancouver Maritime Museum.

BOOKS: *The Original Astronomic Observations made in the course of a voyage to the Northern Pacific Ocean* (London, 1782).

JAMES TREVENEN

Fascination with Cook's final voyage is such that journalistic works and books have continued to be published for centuries afterwards. Born in 1760, James Trevenen was a midshipman on the *Resolution* and later on the *Discovery*. A manuscript volume of his nautical notes resides in the Provincial Archives of Victoria. They form the basis for a Navy Records Society volume that varies slightly from the Provincial Archives version. After Cook's death, Trevenen annotated his own copy of James King's volume of the official version of the voyage. He later sailed with his friend Captain James King in the West Indies and died in military action against the Swedes in 1790 after he took a commission as captain in the Russian navy. He made his will in St. Petersburg

The Discovery *and* Resolution *at Resolution Cove, Bligh Island, Nootka Sound, April 1778. By M.B. Messer, based on a drawing by John Webber.*

just prior to the engagement. His brother-in-law, the Vice-Admiral Sir Charles V. Penrose, took Trevenen's diary notes of Cook's voyage and published them after his death. This Penrose manuscript is at the National Maritime Museum in Greenwich.

BOOKS: *A Memoir of James Trevenen*, eds. Christopher Lloyd & R.C. Anderson (London: Navy Records Society, vol. CI, 1959).

———◈———

GEORGE GILBERT

G eorge Gilbert's writing has been lauded as even-handed, even
mature, reminiscent of the "magnificent lack of imagina-
tion" displayed by the younger James Cook in his *Endeavour* journal.

George Gilbert joined Captain Cook's 1776 expedition as a
seaman and was promoted to midshipman during the voyage.
His father George Gilbert had served as master on the the *Resolution* for its preceding voyage to the Pacific, during which time
Cook had named Gilbert Island off the coast of Tierra del Fuego
for him. Upon his father's retirement, John Gilbert had been
replaced as master by William Bligh, later deposed as captain
during the mutiny on the *Bounty*.

While in his late teens or early twenties, Gilbert was on the
Resolution when Cook visited Nootka Sound and undertook repairs from late March 1778 until April 27. His extensive account
of their travels was not included within *The Journals of Captain
Cook. Vol. 3. Parts 1 & 2, Resolution and Discovery*—as were extracts
from journals by his contemporaries Anderson, Clerke, Burney,
Williamson, Edgar and King—because Gilbert's 325-page manuscript journal was likely completed in the early 1780s.

Gilbert's memoir was not published until two centuries later,
80 years after a descendant of Gilbert's brother, Richard Gilbert,
took the manuscript to the British Museum in 1912.

At King George Sound, Gilbert described the perceived threat
of attack by two large parties of canoes. Cook was unwilling to
fire at them. "At last we discovered it to be a quarral betwixt the
two parties, and that the dispute was the right of trading with us;
which after several long harangues, and threatening gestures, on
both sides, was happily decided without their proceeding to

greater extremities: and both parties traided with us ever afterwards in a very peaceable manner, and friendly," Gilbert recalled. "They had very often little quarrels with one another alongside, which generally ended with pulling each others hair; this they would do for near half an hour together, without the least motion till one of them gave out, being apparently of a very obstinate dispossion. When their disputes do not run so high as to require weapons to decide them, this seems to be the only method they make us[e] of; having no idea of striking with their hands, which is rather surprizing, as boxing is generally practiced by most Indians."

When the *Resolution* and *Discovery* returned to Kealakekua Bay in Hawaii on January 17, 1779, some of the Hawaiians initially believed—so the story goes—that Captain Cook could be the ancient God Lono returned to them. It had been foretold that Lono would return on large floating islands. Nevertheless, so many islanders tried to board the *Discovery* that that there was a danger of capsizing.

"When we wanted to work," Gilbert wrote, "we could not come at the ropes without first driving the greater part of them [the Hawaiians] overboard; which they bore with the utmost cheerfulness and good nature jumping from every part of the ship into the water, as fast as they could, appearing to be much diverted at it, and would come on board again when the business was over."

When Captain James Cook was killed at Kealakekua Bay, George Gilbert recorded how Cook's men felt when one of them confirmed that they had "lost their father."

"When on the return of the boats informing us of the Captains Death; a general silence ensued throughout the ship, for the space of near half an hour;—it appearing to us some what like a dream that we cou'd not reconcile our selves to for some time. Greif was visible in evry Countenance; Some expressing it by tears; and others by a kind of Gloomy dejection: more easy to be conceived than described: for us all our hopes centrd in him; our loss became irrepairable and the Sense of it was so deeply

Nuu-chah-nulth box
lid, collected 1778,
Vancouver Island.

impressed upon our minds as not to be for-
got."

After Cook's death, Gilbert transferred to
the *Discovery* under Captain Clerke and was
paid off at Woolwich on October 21, 1780.
He became fifth lieutenant on the warship
Magnificent until 1783. The year and nature
of his death are not known. Gilbert's original journal is in the British Museum.

BOOKS: George Gilbert, *The Death of Captain Cook*
(Honolulu: Hawaiian Historical Society Reprints, No.
5., 1926); Christine Holmes, *Captain Cook's Final Voy-
age: The Journal of Midshipman George Gilbert* (Horsham:
Sussex: Caliban Books, 1982; University of Hawaii
Press, 1982).

Chief "Macquena," 1837

Chief Maquinna was the most influential person in the sea otter fur trade of the 18th century on Vancouver Island. After drawing Maquinna wearing a hat that depicted whale hunting [above], Tomás de Suría noted in 1791 that there were three leading "Tais" (chiefs) in Nootka, "the greatest of all in many respects is Maquinna, whose father died [after 1778] in a war against the Tla-umac." Francis Simpkinson, an eighteen-year-old midshipman, depicted a Chief "Macquena" [insert] in 1837. Mike Maquinna is the hereditary spokesperson for the Nuu-chah-nulth in Nootka Sound in the 21st century.

V

TRADERS

James Strange
Alexander Walker
John MacKay
Frances Barkley
John Meares
George Dixon
Nathaniel Portlock
John Nicol
William Beresford
James Colnett
Esteban José Martínez*
Andrew Bracey Taylor

*not a trader

JAMES STRANGE

The first notification in English that large profits were to be made trading sea otter skins was supplied by John Ledyard who recalled that skins brought by Cook's crew from the North Pacific "were of nearly double the value at Canton, as at Kamchatka." The rush to the Pacific Northwest that ensued for four decades was to obtain the pelts of the sea otter (*Enhydra lutris*), the only member of the genus *Enhydra* and the largest member of the family *Mustelidae*, which includes weasels, skunks and badgers. One sea otter pelt was worth ten beaver pelts.

The first of the fur-trading ships to arrive at Nootka Sound was the 60-ton *Harmon*, renamed the *Sea Otter*, commanded by James Hanna. Its arrival from Macao in August of 1785 marked the onset of the modern economy of British Columbia, an economy based on the exploitation of natural resources for the next two centuries. Hanna's expedition also began two centuries of fractious relations between invasive Europeans and indigenous peoples when, as a practical joke, Hanna and his crew of 20 men set off a charge of gun powder under Chief Maquinna's chair. After one of the Indians stole a chisel, 20 Indians were killed in an ensuing confrontation. Nonetheless, Hanna's men collected 560 sea otter pelts and sold them for a fortune in China in December 1785.

The following year an American commercial trading house was opened in Canton and at least eight fur-trading vessels ventured to the Northwest Coast including a 100-ton ship, also called the *Sea Otter*, commanded by Hanna. The first of these to reach Nootka Sound in 1786 were the 350-ton *Captain Cook* and the 100-ton *Experiment*, commanded by Henry Laurie and Henry Guise respectively, but both under the direction of James Strange.

As an employee of the East India Company usually stationed

Russians began hunting the sea otter in the 1740s and coined the term "soft gold."

in Bombay and Madras, James Strange had read of Captain Cook's voyages while recuperating from an illness in Britain. He persuaded Bombay merchant David Scott partially to finance his expedition to Nootka Sound. With Strange aboard the *Captain Cook*, the traders embarked from Bombay on December 8, 1785, and gathered more supplies at Batavia. They reached Vancouver Island on June 25, 1786, near Hope Bay. They anchored at Friendly Cove on July 7.

A soldier aboard the *Experiment*, Alexander Walker, dealt extensively with the Indians and kept a journal, but James Strange kept aloof, preferring negotiations with an older chief named Kurrighum rather than Maquinna. One of the numerous crewmen who were ill, John MacKay, or Mackey, an assistant surgeon aboard the *Experiment*, was voluntarily left behind when the two ships sailed north with 540 sea otter pelts.

Strange named the islands at the north end of Vancouver Island the Scott Islands and Cape Scott in dedication to his financier David Scott. He also named Queen Charlotte Sound. After entering Prince William Sound, Strange was surprised to meet yet another vessel named the *Sea Otter*, this one a trading vessel from Calcutta, commanded by William Tipping, who later disappeared with his ship en route to Cook Inlet, never to be seen again. The Strange expedition left Prince William Sound on September 14, 1786. The *Experiment* reached Macao in mid-November; the *Captain Cook* reached Asia in December. Strange's expedition was not a financial success. He died in 1840.

James Charles Stewart Strange was born in London in 1753 and was named by his godfather, Bonnie Prince Charlie. His early visit to Vancouver Island has long since been overshadowed by the more significant voyages of others, but he is credited with planting the first European vegetables on the Northwest Coast.

After a five-year search, B.A. McKelvie and W.M. Halliday claimed to have found a copper cylinder in a tree on Nigei Island in 1933, having ascertained its whereabouts from Strange's journal that was published in India in the 1920s.

BOOKS: James Strange, *Journal and Narrative of the Commercial Expedition from Bombay to the Northwest Coast of America* (Madras, India: Government Record Office, 1928; A.V. Ayyar, *An Adventurous Madras Civilian, James Strange* (Calcutta, 1929); eds. A.V. Venkatarama Ayyar, John Hosie, & F.W. Howay, *James Strange's Journal and Narrative of the Commercial Expedition from Bombay to the Northwest Coast of America: With Introductory Material* (Ye Galleon Press, 1982).

ALEXANDER WALKER

"The Savage, who is nevertheless dishonest, pretends to be Scrupulous, and exact in his dealings." —ALEXANDER WALKER

Ensign Alexander Walker sailed with Captain James Charles Stewart Strange to Nootka Sound eight years after Captain Cook's visit. Editors Robin Fisher and J.M. Bumsted have suggested that, "While Strange's Journal is concerned with trade and self-justification, Walker's account is the product of the scientific curiosity that brought so many explorers to the Pacific."

Some of the Chinook vocabulary that evolved along the Pacific Coast can be traced to initial contacts between the Nuu-chah-nulth and interpreters such as Walker in 1785. His original journal was lost but he reconstructed his account between 1813 and 1831. That work remained unpublished until 1982. It was rediscovered in the Scottish National Library in the late 20th century. The memoir reflects Walker's sometimes condescending perspective in 1785 and 1786 as he struggled to bridge the language barrier amid earnest efforts to learn.

"They were [so] much dissatisfied, with the shape of our tools, that they generally altered it after buying them."
—Alexander Walker, 1785

"[Nootka]," he believed, "is nearly... deficient in pronouns, and entirely wants the Article. For instance, Mokquilla [Chief Maquinna]... in place of expressing himself in this way, I killed a Sea Otter, he would say, *Mokquilla kakhsheetl quotluk*, Mokquilla kill Sea Otter. The want of personal pronouns is sometimes supplied by signs. We often observed these People at a loss for words to explain their sentiments, particularly in subjects that were not immediately before their senses, or when they talked of past or future events. We may trace in those circumstances the speech and simplicity of Infants. A Savage is Man in a state of Infancy. These Americans speak in short sentences, and one word seems frequently to express a compleat proposition. They showed no desire to become acquainted with any more of our language than the words, Copper and Iron. But they were prevented from acquiring even these, by a total inability of pronouncing the letter R; in place of which they always substituted L."

Walker's transcriptions into English of the dialect known as Mowachaht are accurate enough to allow contemporary speakers of the language to identify most of the words he recorded. For example, *Kishkiltup* is strawberry; *Klooweekmubt* is tasteless red berry; *Takna* is child; *Keymeess* is blood; *Wakoo* is urine. More than a dozen Nuu-chah-nulth dialects are spoken between Bamfield and Cape Cook on Vancouver Island. The two Nuu-chah-nulth groups at Nootka Sound were the Mowachaht and the Muchalaht. The Vancouver Island Tribal Council adopted the name Nuu-chah-nulth in 1980 to refer to all indigenous people on the west coast of Vancouver Island. It means "all along the mountains."

Walker's journal contains one of the earliest written accusations that some of Maquinna's people were cannibals. He, like other sailors and traders, was offered a severed hand as an item of great value. After Walker enquired as to its purpose, the woman offering the hand bit into Walker's arm. Spanish and English expeditions often recorded how the legs and arms of children were brought to their ships for sale. Walker surmised cannibalism at Nootka was not "for the sake of food" but "was apparently confined to the devouring [of] their Enemies and probably some choice bits only were selected." Historian and editor Robin Fisher has concluded, "Clearly the Nootka did engage in ritual cannibalism for dramatic effect. Arm biting and the display of hands and skulls of slain enemies were all part of Nootka ceremonial. But this does not mean that human flesh was actually devoured."

Alexander Walker was born on May 12, 1764 in Fife, Scotland, the eldest of five children, and the son of a Church of Scotland minister who died in 1771. Although he was able to attend university, the poverty of his family forced him to work as a cadet for the East India Company. Promoted to ensign in 1782, he fought against Hyder Ali in Malabar, distinguishing himself when he offered to surrender as a hostage. Walker was encouraged to accompany James Strange's proposed expedition by the Bombay Council. He later wrote, "I thought that I could not employ myself better, than visiting a Country little known, which might afford many objects of curiousity."

Walker was not impressed by his captain but refrained from overtly criticizing Strange in his journal. Walker later had a distinguished career as a soldier and administrator in India, participating in a campaign with the governor of Bombay to eradicate female infanticide. Walker matured into a scholar of Hinduism, publishing several papers, and increasingly defending the rights of indigenous peoples. He passed a decade in retirement on an estate in the Scottish Border Country before serving as Governor of St. Helena (1822–1828). He died in 1831.

BOOKS: *An Account of a Voyage to the Northwest Coast of America in 1785 & 1786 by Alexander Walker*, eds. R. Fisher & J.A. Bumsted (Douglas & McIntyre, 1982).

JOHN MACKAY

"The testimony of McKoy [MacKay]...leaves the fact in doubt whether these people are really cannibals." —ALEXANDER WALKER

If anyone was ever in an ideal position to provide a reliable opinion as to whether or not the Mowachaht ate human flesh beyond ritualistic (symbolic) cannibalism, it was John MacKay— the first European to suggest that Vancouver Island is an island.

Captured by Maquinna in the early 19th century, the famous John Jewitt ("White Slave of the Nootka") was not the first year-round European resident of British Columbia. That distinction belongs to MacKay, the young, Irish-born, Bombay soldier who sailed with Captains Henry Laurie and Henry Guise during the Strange expedition that arrived at Nootka Sound on June 27, 1786. Due to an illness described as "purple fever," MacKay was left behind to live with the Mowachaht Chief Maquinna in 1786–87. Since he had somehow managed to cure Maquinna's daughter Apenas of a "scabby disease," the quasi-physician was initially well-treated. He regained his health and initially adapted well.

Supplied with two goats, some seeds and a gun, MacKay also had ink and paper to record "every Occurrence, however trivial, which might serve to throw any Light on our hitherto confined knowledge of the Manners, Customs, Religion and Government of these people." But after elderly Chief Kurrigham tore up his writing materials, the first amateur ethnologist in B.C. was unable to complete the task. MacKay nonetheless felt sufficiently well-entrenched, having been promised a wife by Maquinna, to decline an offer from Captain Hanna in 1786 to leave Nootka Sound ahead of schedule. MacKay told Hanna that he was confident his supercargo James Strange would make the necessary arrangements to retrieve him, as promised.

He should have accepted Captain Hanna's offer. MacKay allowed the Mowachaht to dismantle his musket, then he was unable to retrieve the pieces. "Deprived of this powerful Weapon of respect," Alexander Walker reported, "he became less formidable, and less secure." More trouble arose when he unwittingly stepped over the cradle of Maquinna's child, thereby breaking a local taboo. MacKay was beaten and banished for weeks. When Maquinna's infant died, MacKay was exiled from Maquinna's house to survive on his own. "It was impossible after this," reported Walker, "to recover the Confidence and esteem of Mokquilla." When the village moved for the winter, MacKay was barely able to feed himself. He ate the seeds in his possession and came down with the "bloody flux." In the spring, still ostracized, he mainly had dealings with women and children. "His Skill in Medicine stood him in little stead," said Walker. "This Profession too was in the Hands of their Women, whose knowledge of Simples and Herbs, Mackoy mentioned to be extensive." MacKay witnessed a horrible massacre of about twelve captive men on the beach. This was later described at length by Walker.

Upon the arrival of the *Imperial Eagle* in June of 1787, MacKay gladly agreed to serve as Captain Charles Barkley's guide, translator and sales agent to help him acquire sea otter furs. Trading went well. Trouble arose only when two more English ships arrived at Friendly Cove about one month later and discovered Barkley had obtained the best pelts at the best prices. Having embarked from England before the *Imperial Eagle* had left Ostend, the crews of both the *Prince of Wales* and the sloop *Princess Royal*

Before he was beaten and banished, the Irishman John MacKay shared a house like this one with Maquinna at Yuquot in Nootka Sound. From a drawing by John Webber of the Cook expedition.

were already feeling disadvantaged. Both ships had been delayed due to scurvy. The captains of the *Prince of Wales* and the sloop *Princess Royal* were not charitably disposed to learn the *Imperial Eagle* had not only been renamed and refitted at a foreign port, it was flying under Austrian colours to avoid paying the high fees demanded by the Asian monopoly of the East India Company. Taking umbrage, Captains Colnett and Duncan noted the fundamental role that MacKay had played at their expense. The brother of the owner of the *Prince of Wales*, a certain "Mr. Etches," was on board the expedition, in charge of cargo, and it was Etches who reported MacKay's complicity to Captain George Dixon. Upon hearing the news of illegal trading, Dixon intended to take MacKay back to Canton in irons, and charge him with poaching, but in the end he could not catch him.

Captain George Dixon's journal recorded the biased views of "Mr. Etches" concerning MacKay. "His name is John M'Key; he was born in Ireland.... The *Sea Otter* under Captain Hanna, from China, arrived at King George's Sound in August, 1786, and that Captain Hanna offered to take him on board, which he refused, alledging, that he began to relish dried fish and whale oil, was satisfied with his way of life, and perfectly contented to stay 'til next year, when he had no doubt of Mr. Strange sending for him: That Captain Hanna left the Sound in September. That the natives had stripped him of his cloaths, and obliged him to adopt their mode of dress and filthiness of manners; and that he was now a perfect master of their language, and well acquainted with their temper and disposition. He had made frequent incursions into the interior parts of the country about King George's Sound, and did not think any part of it was the Continent of America, but a chain of detached islands.... Mr. Etches (from whom I had this intelligence) assured me that no great dependence could be placed on M'Key's story, he being a very ignorant young fellow, and frequently contradicting himself; but that entire credit might be given to that part of it respecting his adopting the manners of the natives, as he was equally slovenly and dirty with the filthiest of them all. His knowledge of the language was greatly short of what he boasted; neither was he very contented in his situation, for he gladly embraced Captain Barkley's offer of taking him on board, and seemed delighted to think he was going to leave so uncomfortable a place: however, admitting him to be possessed of but an ordinary capacity, he certainly must be better acquainted with the people here, from more than a year's residence amongst them, than any occasional visitor could possibly be; and there can be no doubt but that Captain Barkley found him extremely useful in managing his traffic with the natives."

MacKay was never prosecuted by Captain Dixon. He succeeded in reaching the Orient with Captain Barkley, then made his way to India. One of his former shipmates, Alexander Walker, found him in Bombay in 1788, much the worse for wear, a shattered man suffering from alcoholism. Nonetheless, MacKay was the first European to reside at Nootka during an entire winter when the Mowachaht held their most important ceremonies at Tahsis, so

Walker sought whatever information he could gain.

Walker reported, "He was of the opinion that they did not actually devour their captives and slain enemies. They only washed their hands in their blood and tasted it. The dried hands he insisted were preserved as trophies and charms.... The testimony of McKoy [MacKay] must be admitted of superior weight to our cursory observations and it at least leaves the fact in doubt whether these people are really cannibals."

A less than sympathetic interviewer, Alexander Walker contrived the following recollection of his conversation with MacKay in Bombay.

Q: How long did the Savages remain at Friendly Village after the departure of the Vessel?

A: The Savages remained about three weeks at the Village, after the departure of the Vessels from the Sound.

Q: Whither did they proceed after they quitted the Village?

A: They directed their course up the Sound, about Thirty Miles, distant from where the Vessels were Moored.

Q: When did they return to the Village?

A: They returned no more to the Village at the Mouth of the Sound until the Close of the ensuing Winter.

Q: What motives had they for leaving the Sea Coast?

A: Their motives for leaving the Sea Coast were to provide a more comfortable retreat in the Winter, and also to supply themselves with a large kind of Fish resembling make and size a Salmon, which came up the Rivers to Spawn, and which they take in vast quantities; it is these Fish when Smoke dried without Salt, and Porpoise Oil, that constitute their Food when the Severity of the Season will not admit of their going out of doors. Their Amusements are few, and may be considered rather Trials of Strength than of Skill.

Q: What Animals did they choose to obtain on their hunting incursions?

A: The Animals most commonly taken on their hunting parties are Bear, Mousedeer, Racoon, and Martin. The Skin of which is next in Estimation to that of the Sea Otter; the Bear is harpoon'd, and some times intraped, which is done by placing a double row of Stones about 2 feet High in a Semicircular form with a cross bar in the Centre, which falls on his Neck when he pulls the bait that is made fast to it by a string, at which time they take the advantage to rush out in a body and soon dispatch him.

Nootka noblewoman and child depicted by Atanasio Echeverría in 1792. "I am well convinced the Modesty of their Women proceeds rather from a Principal of the Mind, than a fear of their Husbands." – John MacKay.

Q: How do they catch the Sea Otter?

A: The Sea Otter is exceedingly shy and confined to the Water. Its' food is on Fish; when it is wounded by the Arrow his utmost endeavours are to free himself from it, while in the mean time the Natives strike him with a harpoon before he goes down under the Water.

Q: What became of the Goats left with you?

A: The Goats left me by Mr. Strange died during the Inclemency of the Season for want of Food.

Q: What Accidents befell you during the time you staid among these People?

A: I was taken ill about the Middle of October with a flux, which continued for near 3 Weeks, and before I had regained my strength was attacked with a putrid Fever, which I cannot with any degree of certainty tell how long it lasted, being deprived of my Senses, nor do I know in what manner the Natives had treated me.

The diseases in general with which they died of arose from indigestion, the Women especially are more subject to Complaints in the Bowels than either Men or Children, (which I suppose proceeds from eating heartily and taking little exercise).

Q: Can you give an Account of any Institutions which appeared to you remarkable?

A: Their Marriage Ceremonies are performed by addressing the Chief of the district to which they belong at the same time accompanied by a small present, (of either Copper or Iron) informing him of the object of choice which he fails not to [procure] them. Their Women seldom or ever prove incontinent to their Husbands, nor do I think in case they did so would it make any material difference to them. They believe in a future state of existence.

Q: Did the Women appear under restraint in the particular above mentioned?

A: I am well convinced the Modesty of their Women proceeds rather from a Principal of the Mind, than a fear of their Husbands. It is an uncommon Circumstance for Girls to be [naked] before Marriage.

BOOKS: Alexander Walker, *A Voyage Round the World: But More Particularly to the North West Coast of America* (London: George Dixon, 1789); Alexander Walker, *An Account of a Voyage to the North West Coast of America in 1785 & 1786* (Douglas & McIntyre, University of Washington Press, 1982).

FRANCES BARKLEY

The first European woman to visit British Columbia was Frances Barkley who arrived with her husband in 1787 at age eighteen. She was also the first woman to write about British Columbia. Almost two centuries later, her memoirs entitled *Reminiscences* were published within *The Remarkable World of Frances Barkley 1769–1845*, edited by Beth Hill (Gray's, 1978).

As well, Frances Barkley has the little-known distinction of being the first woman known to have sailed, openly as a woman, around the world. Jeanne Baret, a Frenchwoman, had accompanied her lover, Philibert de Commerson, a botanist, during the first French expedition to circumnavigate the globe in 1769, but she had to disguise herself as a male valet in order to do so. Her female identity was discovered part way through the scientific voyage that was completed by Louis Antoine de Bougainville.

Similarly, the Frenchwoman Rose de Freycinet successfully conspired with her husband Louis-Claude de Freycinet to accompany him as a stowaway on his scientific voyage around the world on the *Uranie* in 1817–1820.

Frances Barkley was born in Bridgewater, Somersetshire, England in 1769, as Frances Hornby Trevor, daughter of an English chaplain who had moved his family to Europe in 1775 and become rector of a new Protestant Church at Ostend in 1783. Educated at a French Catholic convent, she was a student of French who also learned sewing, embroidery and cooking. One of her sisters married Captain James Cook. At age seventeen, she married twenty-six-year-old sea captain Charles William Barkley on October 17, 1786, at Ostend.

The young Captain Barkley opted to sail under the Austrian colours of the Austrian East Indian Company in an attempt to circumvent the high fees demanded by the two English monopolies. These were the East India Company, Charles Barkley's former employer, and the South Sea Company. The former controlled trade in Asia; the latter controlled the Pacific trade on the West Coast of North America from Cape Horn to the Arctic.

The name of Barkley's ship, the *Loudon,* was changed to the *Imperial Eagle* prior to the couple's embarkation on November 24, 1786. Despite a bout of rheumatic fever for Captain Barkley, their voyage went well, and they soon reached the South American coast at Brazil.

At the Sandwich Islands Frances Barkley took aboard a maidservant, Winée, who became the first Hawaiian or "Kanaka" to reach British Columbia. Few details are known about her life. She sailed with the Barkleys to Nootka Sound, then onto China, but in Macao she wanted to return to Hawaii. She was given re-

Imperial Eagle, *largest ship in Friendly Cove, pre-1800.*

turn passage to Nootka Sound on a voyage by Captain John Meares in the spring of 1788. He described her as being "in a deep decline." Winée died en route on February 5, 1788 and her body was committed to the deep.

The Barkleys arrived in the *Imperial Eagle* at Nootka Sound in June of 1787. At 400 tons, the *Imperial Eagle* was the largest ship to enter Friendly Cove but the Indians were likely just as impressed by Frances Barkley's extraordinary red-gold hair. Legend has it, within Barkley family lore, that her tresses saved the day when the Barkleys were captured by hostile South Sea natives. The story goes that curious women among their captors supposedly loosed her hair "which fell like a shower of gold," whereupon the astonished onlookers presumed she must be divine and Frances successfully ordered their release. This incident does not appear in any of Frances Barkley's diary materials. Her cumulative *Reminiscences* were mostly penned when she was sixty-six.

During their month-long stay at Nootka, Frances Barkley was

much impressed by chief Maquinna and his management of the fur trade. The *Imperial Eagle* acquired 700 prime skins, and many more of inferior quality, worth a great fortune for sale in the Orient. They did so with the assistance of John MacKay, the Irishman who had been left behind at Nootka the summer before due to illness. The Barkleys sailed south and named Barkley Sound, Hornby Peak, Frances Island, Trevor Channel, Loudoun Channel, Cape Beale and Imperial Eagle Channel. In honour of the local chief, Captain Barkley also named Wickinninish Sound, now called Clayoquot Sound. Six of their party were killed by Indians at the mouth of the Strait of Juan de Fuca on July 24, 1787. Depressed by this encounter, the Barkleys set sail for Canton and reached Macao in December.

During formal trading procedures in Macao—which proved successful—the Barkleys bought an ornate bamboo chair that has survived their journeys. This chair is now the property of the Centennial Museum in Vancouver.

Having made a profit of £10,000 for his backers, Captain Barkley proceeded to the island of Mauritius, off Madagascar, where he learned the East India Company was initiating legal action against the owners of the *Imperial Eagle*. The owners, who included John Meares, decided to sell the *Imperial Eagle* to avoid legal consequences, thereby breaking their contract with Captain Barkley. The Barkleys stayed for more than a year in the French enclave of Mauritius where Frances Barkley gave birth to their first child, a son. Captain Barkley sailed to India where the *Imperial Eagle* was confiscated. Having invested much of his own money in properly outfitting the ship, Captain Barkley sued for damages and received an arbitration settlement for the loss of his ten-year contract but this was insufficient consolation.

The devious Meares gained possession of Barkley's nautical gear as well as his valuable seafaring journal. "Capt. Meares, however, with the greatest effrontery," Frances Barkley later wrote, "published and claimed the merit of my husband's discoveries therein contained, besides inventing lies of the most revolting nature tending to vilify the person he thus pilfered." The likes of

Robert Haswell and George Dixon also condemned Meares when his book about his adventures failed to properly credit Captain Barkley's charts. It was, according to Dixon, "scarcely anything more than a confused heap of contradictions and misrepresentations." For his part, chief Maquinna, a shrewd judge of character, called Meares "*Aita-aita Meares*" which means "the lying Meares." Defrauded by Meares and stranded in Mauritius, having lost the *Imperial Eagle,* and also burdened with a newborn, the Barkleys tried to return to England on an American ship that was wrecked near Holland where they were left to fend for themselves. They finally reached Portsmouth two years after their embarkation from Ostend.

Modern historian Beth Hill retrieved Frances Barkley from obscurity.

Undeterred, the Barkleys conceived a second voyage seven months later, to be made to Alaska via India. During their eleven-month voyage to Calcutta aboard the *Princess Frederica,* Frances Barkley gave birth to a baby girl during a violent gale while rounding the Cape of Good Hope in 1791. "Nothing would be easy in this environment; even washing diapers presented a challenge," her biographer Beth Hill wrote. "Fresh water was always at a premium so washing in saltwater would be the norm. Salt-encrusted diapers would have caused boils and open sores which do not heal easily, and infection often followed."

The Barkleys left Calcutta on December 29, 1791, having purchased the 80-ton brig *Halcyon* and a smaller accompanying vessel, the *Venus.* Frances Barkley had the option of remaining in Bengal "where I was to have Servants, Palanqueens and every Luxery," but she resolutely insisted on accompanying her husband, "much to the satisfaction of My Husband, who never thought of being separated from me." Others called it madness. The infant at her breast would die "and became the Victim of our folly" during this second voyage. "A Leaden Box was prepared for her remains in order that they be kept until we could Inter her in consicrated ground in some Dutch settlement," Frances Barkley wrote.

It was no picnic for the crew either. Many sailors died due to foul conditions. "Typhus and dysentery were the shore diseases of Europe," wrote Beth Hill, "and in the tropics the seamen got malaria, yellow fever, hookworm and typhus. Lice and fleas were taken for granted, and the lice carried typhus. Venereal diseases were considered an occupational ailment of sailors and in the 18th century, treatment was ineffective. In port...boatloads of prostitutes were ferried to the ship; the scene below decks can be imagined and it is not surprising that syphilis and gonorrhea were widespread." Killing someone often resulted in the guilty party being tied to the victim and thrown overboard.

Attempts to trade in Siberia during this second voyage were stymied by Russian officialdom. They also met resistance when they entered the ancestral waters of the unpredictable and often fearsome Tlingit. Nonetheless Frances Barkley became the first European woman to visit Alaska in 1792. They wintered at "the island of Oyhee" (Hawaii) but the voyage of the *Halcyon* went from bad to worse.

Having gained fewer pelts than hoped, the Barkleys reached China in March of 1793 and sailed to Mauritius—unaware that France and England were once again at war. The French confiscated the *Halcyon* and the Barkleys temporarily became prisoners. An American sailed the *Halcyon* to the United States while the Barkleys remained on Mauritius.

They eventually found a ship to take them to the United States but by then their own ship could not be traced. They reached England in November of 1794 on the *Amphion*. Learning the *Halcyon* was in Boston, Captain Barkley returned there and regained ownership of the vessel. The Barkleys subsequently raised a family in England where Captain Barkley died on May 16, 1832.

Four years later in 1836, Frances Barkley began writing her fragmented memoirs. The manuscript of *Reminiscences*—mostly written from memory—is housed at the Provincial Archives in Victoria. Beth Hill discovered the manuscript while researching a book on petroglyphs. At that time Hill knew only that Frances Barkley was eighteen years old when she came to British Columbia on her honeymoon.

Soon she found herself back in the archives, reading the other letters and documents in the Barkley files, the article by Captain Walbran entitled "The Cruise of the Imperial Eagle" and the discussion of the mystery of the missing Diary of Frances Barkley by W. Kaye Lamb in the *British Columbia Historical Journal.*

"I was surprised that I had read so little of the Barkley story elsewhere," Beth Hill wrote.

In 1901, Captain John T. Walbran, a coastal surveyor and author of an essential study of place names of B.C., had researched an article for the *Victoria Colonist* about the first voyage of the Barkleys based on his access to Frances Barkley's original sea diary—not the *Reminiscenses.* This diary was presumed to have been burned in a house fire at Westholme on Vancouver Island in 1909, but Hill later uncovered some evidence to suggest it might have existed until about 1953. Walbran's article provides essential details about Captain Barkley's explorations that were not included in Frances Barkley's *Reminiscences.*

During her two voyages with her husband, Frances Barkley spent a total of six-and-a-half years at sea, losing one child in the process, but there is not a single complaint in her memoir about the conditions and disappointments she endured. Her vigour can only be imagined.

She died in 1845.

BOOKS: *The Remarkable World of Frances Barkley, 1769–1845*, ed. Beth Hill (Sidney, British Columbia: Gray's Publishing, 1978); *The Remarkable World of Frances Barkley, 1769–1845*, eds. Beth Hill and Cathy Converse (Heritage House, 2003); **MANUSCRIPTS:** Charles W. Barkley's "Log of Imperial Eagle, 1786–1787"; Charles W. Barkley's "Log of the Halcyon, 1792."

JOHN MEARES

"In their characters they are reserved and chaste; and examples of loose and immodest conduct were very rare among them." —JOHN MEARES

John Meares has been described as the Machiavelli of the maritime fur trade. As the Englishman most responsible for exaggerating the Nootka Incident, he was an untrustworthy conniver who built the first European residence in British Columbia in 1788 and oversaw construction of the first European-designed boat to be built in British Columbia, the *North West America,* using Chinese labour.

Born around 1756, and having served in the Royal Navy, Meares was one of many Englishmen who hoped to establish trade in sea otter furs to Japan. On behalf of the Bengal Fur Society, Meares sailed from Calcutta, then Madras, in March of 1786 on the *Nootka.* The Bengal Fur Company was newly formed in January of 1786 by a group of merchants headed by J.H. Cox, supposedly with the approval of the East India Company and Sir John Macpherson, Governor-General of India.

In tandem with Meares, William Tipping, another former lieutenant in the Royal Navy, was instructed to sail the *Sea Otter* by way of Japan. Meares instructed Tipping "to endeavour to open an amicable Intercourse with the Inhabitants of Corea or Japan, or the Islands to the North or South" after delivering his cargo of opium to Malacca. Meares reached the Aleutian Islands in the summer and spent a desperate winter in Prince William Sound where 23 of his men died.

In October one of his officers traded with the local chief Sheenoway for a young female captive. According to Meares she was acquired in exchange for an ax and a small quantity of beads.

Portrait of the scoundrel John Meares.

Meares wrote, "She remained with us near four months, and appeared to be very contented with her condition." John Meares, the notorious liar, did not mention that the woman later chose to escape rather than remain with the sailors, as recorded by Captains Portlock and Dixon.

Meares' ship was stranded in the ice, and his men continued to die all through the winter. By the spring of 1787, 30 of his crew had scurvy. The ship's surgeon and pilot died and were buried ashore ("the chasms in the ice their graves").

The ill-equipped expedition was rescued by the rival trader Captain George Dixon on May 19, in his ship the *Queen Charlotte*. Meares' ship also gained assistance from Dixon's superior, Captain Nathanial Portlock, aboard the *King George*. Dixon and Portlock, who had sailed with Captain Cook, both took a dislike to Meares, regarding him as illegitimate competition for furs.

When Meares made a return voyage to the Pacific Northwest from Macao in 1788, he did so under Portuguese colours to avoid British East India and South Sea Company restrictions. Meares embarked in January with 50 men on the *Felice Aventurer*. His former partner Tipping had been lost at sea with the *Sea Otter*, so Meares partnered this time with William Douglas who sailed the

157

The first ship built in British Columbia by Europeans was the 40-foot schooner North West America *under the supervision of Robert Funter, one of John Meares' officers. It was launched at Nootka Sound on September 19, 1788.*

Iphigenia Nubiana. The two ships parted company after the Philippines when Douglas headed for Alaskan waters. Douglas arrived in Cook Inlet on June 16, 1788, and did not join Meares at Nootka until August 27, 1788.

Meares reached Nootka Sound on May 13, 1788. Ostensibly in exhange for eight or ten sheets of copper and some trifles, Meares gained permission from Maquinna to establish his base at Friendly Cove. A blacksmith set up a forge and Meares ordered construction of the *North West America.* Later Meares variously claimed to have brought between 50 and 70 Chinese labourers for the shipbuilding project. Esteban Martínez and William Colnett reported there were 29 Chinese: seven carpenters, five blacksmiths, five masons, four tailors, four shoemakers, three sailors and one cook.

Although his ambitions were commercial, Meares recorded some of his own views of the Mowachaht. "In their exterior form they have not the symmetry or elegance which is found in many other Indian nations. Their limbs, though stout and athletic, are crooked and ill-shaped; their skin, when cleansed of filth and ochre, is white, and we have seen some of the women, when in a state of cleanliness, which, however, was by no means a common sight, and obtained with difficulty, who not only possessed the fair complexion of Europe, but features that would have attracted notice for their delicacy and beauty, in those parts of the world where the qualities of the human form are best understood....

"Their hair, like that of the men, is black; their eyes are of the same color; and, in their exterior appearance, they are not to be immediately distinguished from the men. In their characters they are reserved and chaste; and examples of loose and immodest conduct were very rare among them."

Meares supplied weaponry to Maquinna, tried to discourage his new American trading rivals with false information, and embarked with his furs on the *Felice* for China in September of 1788.

In 1789, trading vessels sent by Meares and his new partners in the Associated Merchants of London and India were seized at Nootka Sound by Captain Martínez, resulting in the Nootka Incident. Captain Colnett and his crew of the *Argonaut* were forced to sail to San Blas as prisoners. Martínez also captured the *North West America* and renamed it *Santa Gertrudis la Magna*.

Back in England, Meares won reparations from Spain for his losses and he stirred anti-Spanish sentiment by publishing unreliable reports. In addition to hastening a diplomatic showdown between Spain and Great Britain, Meares strenuously argued that China, Japan and Korea ought to be considered as markets for British woollens and other manufactured goods, especially since the Dutch were already sending four ships per year to Nagasaki.

Meares died in 1809, loathed by Captain George Dixon who accused him, correctly, of falsifying his seafaring accomplishments and taking credit for the accomplishments of others, particularly Captain Charles Barkley.

Meares Island off Tofino in Clayoquot Sound is named after him.

BOOKS: *Voyages Made in the Years 1788 and 1789 from China to the North West Coast of America* (London, 1790; Amsterdam: N. Israel, 1967).

GEORGE DIXON

"She was what would be reckoned handsome even in England."
—GEORGE DIXON

Captain George Dixon named the Queen Charlotte Islands and was one the first Europeans, after Juan Pérez, to trade with the Haida.

He began his career as an armourer under James Cook aboard the *Discovery* in 1778. He and his partners subsequently formed the King George's Sound Company in 1785 to capitalize on the sea otter trade.

As captain of the ship named *Queen Charlotte*, with Nathaniel Portlock as captain of the *King George*, Dixon had limited success in Alaskan waters in 1786. Both men sailed with necessary licenses from the East India Company. It was during Dixon's second summer spent south of Alaska that he encountered and named the Queen Charlotte Islands after his ship, named for the wife of King George III.

Dixon later left Nootka Sound and traded his furs in China, completing a round-the-world voyage to England in 1788. In his journalistic account of his travels, Dixon included his observations of the Indians he met.

At the village of Yakutat in 1787, he wrote the following extraordinary sentence.

"They, in general, are about middle size, their limbs straight and well-shaped, but like the rest of the inhabitants we have seen on the coast, are particularly fond of painting their faces with a variety of colors so that it is no easy matter to discover their real complexion; however, we prevailed on one woman, by persuasion, and a trifling present, to wash her face and hands, and the alteration it made in her appearance absolutely surprised us; her countenance had all the cheerful glow of an English milk-maid; and the healthy red which flushed her cheek, was even beautifully contrasted with the whiteness of her neck; her eyes were black and sparkling; her eye-brows the same colour, and most beautifully arched; her forehead so remarkably clear, that the translucent veins were seen meandering even in their minutest branches—in short, she was what would be reckoned handsome even in England."

In the same year Dixon described the Haida of the Queen Charlotte Islands. "The people in general are about the middle size, their limbs straight, and tolerable well-shaped; many of the older people are rather lean, but I never saw one person who could be called corpulent amongst them; both sexes are remarkably distinguished by high prominent cheek bones and small eyes....

"In regard to their complexion, it is no easy matter to determine what cast that is; but if I may judge from the few people I saw tolerably clean, these Indians are very little darker than the Europeans in general."

Dixon and Portlock published *A Voyage Round the World: But More Particularly to the North West Coast of America* in London in 1789. Much of the text consisted of 49 letters written by a crew member, William Beresford, and edited by Dixon, who wrote the introduction and appendices. The book was reprinted by Da Capo Press of New York in 1968.

The journal published by Dixon describes the fate of John MacKay, the first European to live year-round in British Columbia. Dixon Entrance north of the Queen Charlotte Islands is named in his honour. Dixon is also connected to the discovery and naming of Port Mulgrave and Norfolk Bay. It is sometimes suggested that Dixon is the same George Dixon who wrote *The Navigator's Assistant* (1791), but there is no proof.

BOOKS: *A Voyage Round the World: But More Particularly to the North West Coast of America, etc.* edited by George Dixon (London: George Goulding, 1789).

NATHANIEL PORTLOCK

In 1785, Nathaniel Portlock sailed from England as captain of the *King George* and explored the Pacific Northwest Coast in the summer of 1786. He wintered in the Sandwich Islands, then became separated from George Dixon of the *Queen Charlotte* in the spring. Portlock sold his furs in China and returned to England in June of 1788, having circumnavigated the world. He joined the British navy in 1788. In 1789, he and Dixon published *A Voyage Round the World* in which Portlock described the coal outcrops near Port Graham, Alaska, which he had named Graham's Harbor. Born circa 1748, he died in London, England, on September 12, 1812.

Nathaniel Portlock

BOOKS: *A Voyage Round the World: But More Particularly to the North West Coast of America etc.* edited by George Dixon (London: George Goulding, 1789).

JOHN NICOL

John Nicol was a sober, Bible-reading man who twice circumnavigated the globe. He was an uncomplicated and observant narrator, although his visit to Nootka Sound did not result in any details.

Born in 1755, he sailed on 12 ships between 1776 and 1801. During his 25 years at sea he visited all six habitable continents.

He served as a cooper aboard Captain Nathaniel Portlock's ship, the *King George,* when it helped rescue John Meares and his stranded crew in Prince William Sound in May of 1787. He described Meares' predicament: "They could not bury their own dead; they were only dragged a short distance from the ship and left upon the ice. They had muskets fixed upon the capstans, and man-ropes that went down to the cabin, that when any of the natives attempted to come on board, they

John Nicol

might fire them off to scare them. They had a large Newfoundland dog, whose name was Towser, who alone kept the ship clear of Indians. He lay day and night upon the ice before the cabin window, and would not allow the Indians to go into the ship. When the natives came to barter, they would cry 'Lally Towser' and make him a present of a skin before they began to trade with Captain Mairs [sic], who lowered from the window his barter and in the same way received their furs."

Nicol visited Hawaii and the Pacific Northwest, befriended slaves in Grenada and recorded their songs, and he documented slavery in Jamaica. While serving aboard a convict ship bound for Australia, he fell in love with Sarah Whitlam, a convict bound for the Botany Bay prison colony. She bore him a son during the year-long voyage but Nicol's seafaring duties forced them apart. Nicol's tour of duty on the *Lady Juliana* has been used as grist for Siân Rees's non-fiction study *The Floating Brothel: The Extraordinary True Story of an Eighteenth-Century Ship and Its Cargo of Female Convicts.* It examines how and why the penal colony in foreign lands was a newly popular alternative to the death penalty.

When Nicol was sixty-seven, his chance encounter with a generous bookbinder, publisher and self-described "polyartist" named John Howell in Edinburgh allowed Nicol, as a destitute sailor, to dictate and publish his memoirs. Howell performed the same task for other working class men of his era. Nicol lived in comfort for the rest of his days, even leaving £30 in his will.

Nicol's story was reprinted by Farrar and Rinehart in 1937, at which time it was claimed it was the earliest memoir by an ordinary sailor that "has any claim to permanence as literature." Upon its reissue in 1999, editor Tim Flannery described Nicol as "not a sailor of the rum, sodomy and lash school."

BOOKS: *The Life and Adventures of John Nicol, Mariner* (1822); *John Nicol's Life and Adventures* (Edinburgh, 1832); *The Life and Adventures of John Nicol, Mariner,* edited by Tim Flannery (*Atlantic Monthly,* 1999).

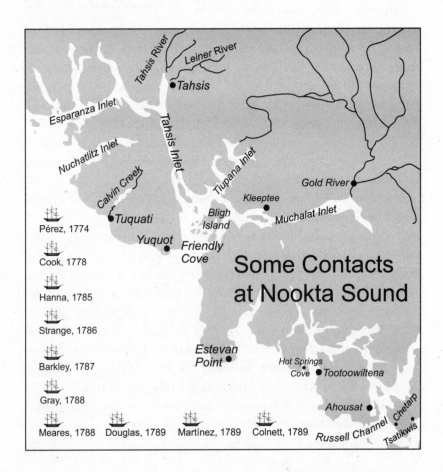

WILLIAM BERESFORD

William Beresford, who sailed as the supercargo under Captain George Dixon on the *Queen Charlotte* in 1785-1787, is seldom credited as the primary author of *A Voyage Round the World* although the work consists largely of letters written by Beresford. Captain Nathaniel Portlock is also credited with the same title.

BOOKS: *A Voyage Round the World: But More Particularly to the North-West Coast of America: Performed in 1785, 1786, 1787 and 1788, in the King George and the Queen Charlotte...* edited by George Dixon (London: George Goulding, 1789).

JAMES COLNETT

"I now saw, but too late, the duplicity of this Spaniard."
—JAMES COLNETT

James Colnett made five Pacific voyages in the late 1700s and early 1800s, over a period of about 13 years, and in the process he became the first European to see parts of the southern Queen Charlotte Islands.

Although Juan Peréz had seen the northern Queen Charlottes [aka Haida Gwaii] in 1774, he hadn't ventured ashore, so Colnett and his crew were among the first Europeans to set foot on the Queen Charlottes. Colnett was also the first Englishman to come in contact with the Tsimshian and the southern Heiltsuk peoples. Despite the achievements of his voyage in 1787–1788, James

Colnett remains more well-known for his one failure than for his successes.

Born in Devon, England, in 1753, Colnett joined the Royal Navy as a seaman in 1770 and gained a posting as a midshipman on the *HMS Scorpion* under Captain Cook in 1771. Rejoining Cook on the *HMS Resolution*, he spent three-and-a-half years under Cook's training during one of the greatest voyages in history. As an experienced navigator, he then negotiated leave from the Admiralty for a commercial enterprise for Richard Cadman Etches & Co. in 1786. In September of that year he embarked from London as commander of a two-vessel expedition to the Northwest Coast of British Columbia in search of furs for trade in China.

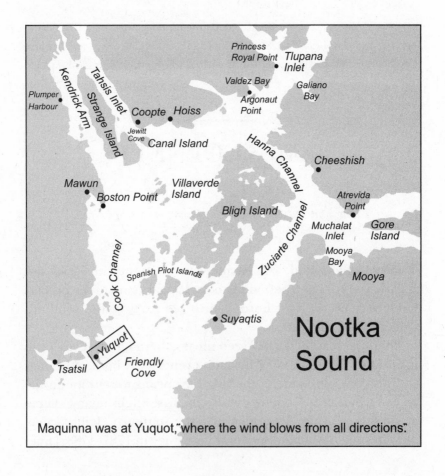

Maquinna was at Yuquot,"where the wind blows from all directions."

He would be absent from England for six years.

Colnett's journal for that period extends to August of 1788 when he departed from the Northwest Coast in the *Prince of Wales*, returning to England via Hawaii and Canton. That journal has been edited by Robert Galois and recently published as *A Voyage to the Northwest Side of America: The Journals of James Colnett, 1786– 89.* Colnett's 182-page account is augmented by extensive notes making for a 441-page book. It contains extracts from a second journal kept by Andrew Bracey Taylor, a third mate on one of the ships under Colnett's command. Although academic in its orientation, the Galois text is far from dull, discussing the trading of sexual favours and other bartering factors.

James Colnett, as much as any Englishman, was directly involved in the Nootka Incident. As captain of the *Argonaut*, Colnett sailed from Macao in April of 1789 and arrived at Nootka Sound on July 3 with instructions to build an English trading post. Colnett's arrival was preceded by the departure of Captain Thomas Hudson in the *Princess Royal.* Astutely interpreting the hostility of Spanish commander Esteban Martínez, Hudson had taken his leave on July 2. The Spanish had already seized Captain William Douglas and the *Iphigenia* on May 12, 1789, holding the crew hostage for several weeks before letting them go.

Colnett refused to recognize the declaration of Spanish sovereignty that was performed by Martínez at Nootka Sound on June 24, 1789. He was determined to build a "solid establishment, and not one that is to be abandoned at pleasure." To be named Fort Pitt, this outpost was to be managed by Robert Duffin (who had sailed with Meares in 1788). With the *Argonaut* moored directly under the Spanish gun placements, Colnett engaged in a furious argument with Martínez on July 4. Colnett's crew was promptly captured and placed ashore, pending their evacuation to Mexico.

Colnett reportedly became unhinged, throwing himself into the water through one of the portholes in his cabin. In a memoir written nine years later, Colnett recalled the circumstances of his arrest.

"On my coming into his cabin, he said he wished to see my

papers; on my presenting them to him, he just glanced his eyes over them, and although he did not understand a word of the language in which they were written, declared they were forged, and threw them disdainfully on the table, saying at the same time, I should not sail until he pleased. On my making some remonstrances at his breach of faith, and his forgetfulness of that word and honour which he had pledged to me, he arose in an apparent anger, and went out.

"I now saw, but too late, the duplicity of this Spaniard, and was conversing with the interpreter on the subject, when having my back towards the cabin door, I by chance cast my eyes on a looking-glass, and saw an armed party rushing behind me. I instantly put my hand to my hanger, but before I had time to place myself in a posture of defence, a violent blow brought me to the ground. I was then ordered into the stocks, and closely confined; after which, they seized my ship and cargo, imprisoned my officers, and put my men in irons.

"They sent their boats likewise to sea and seized the sloop *Princess Royal*, and brought her into port, for trading on the coast. It may not be amiss to observe the Spaniards consider it contrary to treaty, and are extremely jealous, if any European power trades in those seas, but this cannot justify Don Martínez, who, not content with securing me and my people, carried me from ship to ship, like a criminal, rove halter to the yard-arm, and frequently threatened me with instant death, by hanging me as a pirate."

The Spanish made repairs to the *Argonaut* and forced Colnett and his men to sail as prisoners to San Blas. Although they were not harmed, they were kept in custody by the Spanish until May of 1790. Colnett was not permitted to sail from San Blas in the *Argonaut* until July. He sailed north to Clayoquot, resumed trading, and revisited Nootka in 1791. He sailed to the Galapagos Islands in 1792. Spain and England took five years to settle what became known as the Nootka Incident. An agreement was eventually signed at Madrid on January 11, 1794, by the Baron of St. Helens for Great Britain and the Duke of Alcudia for Spain. Both nations agreed to allow each other free access to Nootka Sound.

Colnett sailed to the Pacific again in 1792 on behalf of both the Admiralty and private whaling interests, leading to the development of whaling near the Galapagos Islands. Following his capture and imprisonment in France, Colnett tried convincing the British Admiralty to mount a surprise attack against his Spanish adversaries on the Pacific Coast. Then in 1802 he took more than 400 convicts to Australia. Never married, he died at his lodgings in London in September of 1806.

The journals of Captain James Colnett, ca. 1787–1792, are stored in the Special Collections department of the University of California Library in Los Angeles. *The Journal of Captain James Colnett Aboard the Argonaut from April 26, 1789 to November 3, 1791* includes "A translation of the Diary of Esteban José Martínez from July 2 till July 14, 1789."

BOOKS: *A Voyage to the South Atlantic and Round Cape Horn into the Pacific Ocean* (London, 1798); *The Journal of Captain James Colnett Aboard the Argonaut from April 26, 1789 to November 3, 1791*, ed. F.W. Howay (Toronto: Champlain Society, 1940); *A Voyage to the Northwest Side of America: The Journals of James Colnett, 1786–89*, ed. Robert Galois (Vancouver: UBC Press, 2004).

ESTEBAN JOSÉ MARTÍNEZ

"A zealous but imprudent second-rate explorer."
—HISTORIAN JIM MCDOWELL

Esteban José Martínez, as much as anyone, generated the Nootka Incident that almost resulted in a war between Spain and England. Martínez was the first Spaniard to reside at Nootka Sound and to have extensive relations with the Mowachaht and Nuchatlaht tribes, although his duties were essentially military and he himself was not a trader.

In 1774, Martínez had served as second-in-command for the

first Spanish voyage to reach British Columbia. Having also sailed to the Aleutians in 1788, Martínez was instructed by the Viceroy of New Spain, Manuel Flores, to construct the first permanent outpost of European "civilization" in British Columbia. He was told to make "a large hut" at Nootka Sound and "pretend that you are engaged in setting yourself in a formal establishment."

Martínez arrived at Nootka Sound on May 5, 1789, and was disgruntled from the outset of his stay. He found two American ships were anchored nearby, the *Columbia* and the *Lady Washington*, under John Kendrick and Robert Gray. Even more disconcerting was the presence of the *Iphigenia Nubiana*, a trading vessel under the command of Captain William Douglas. This ship was awaiting the arrival of English trader John Meares.

Wary of both the English and Maquinna, Martínez waited until the arrival of a second Spanish warship, the *San Carlos* under López de Haro, on May 12, before stripping the *Iphigenia* of its trading goods and provisions. Upon completing construction of his new fort, Martínez seized the *North West America* with her furs on June 8, then captured Colnett's *Argonaut* in early July.

Maquinna's son-in-law Callicum took umbrage with the Spanish treatment of the English, whereupon an unintelligible shouting match ensued between Martínez and Callicum on July 13. Martínez tried to shoot Callicum, his gun failed, but a nearby Spanish soldier finished the job.

Esteban José Martínez

Having killed Callicum, the Spanish retained Colnett's Chinese labourers, sent the *Argonaut* and its crew to San Blas, and persuaded Robert Gray to take the crew of the *North West America* to China.

Having gained unrivalled ascendancy, Martínez was surprised to receive new orders to abandon

The first European settlement in British Columbia was begun by Martínez in 1789.

Friendly Cove. In accordance with instructions from the Viceroy of Mexico brought by the supply ship *Aranzazu*, Martínez demolished his fortifications and left in late October.

After John Meares effectively attacked the reputation of Martínez in the courts of Europe, the new Viceroy of New Spain, the Condé de Revilla Gigedo II, instructed Captain Quadra to relieve Martínez of his position.

The Spanish reasserted their position at Nootka Sound in 1790 with Lieutenant Francisco Eliza, assisted by Lieutenant Salvador Fidalgo and Ensign Manuel Quimper.

When Martínez left Nootka Sound, he took with him several young Indians for whom he had bartered their ownership. Christened with Spanish names, they became pawns in an emerging propaganda campaign led by Spanish priests to convince Spanish authorities to commit more funds for missionary conversion of heathen souls. While gathering information from Kendrick, Martínez's pilot José Tobar y Tamiriz had been told that Chief Maquinna kept young prisoners of war who were sometimes butchered and bartered in pieces.

One of the four priests with the Martínez expedition subsequently reported, as recorded in Warren L. Cook's *Flood Tide of Empire:* "Maquinna ate the little boys among the enemies who had the misfortune to fall prisoner. For this purpose he tried to fatten them up first, and then when they were ready, got them all together in a circle (he did this eight days before our people left that waterway), put himself in the middle with an instrument in hand and, looking at all the miserables with furious visage, decided which one was to serve as dish for his inhumane meal. Then, advancing upon the unhappy victim of his voracious appetite, he opened its abdomen at one blow, cut off the arms, and commenced devouring the innocent's raw flesh, bloodying himself as he satiated his barbarous appetite."

A murderous incident in Vespucci's voyage of 1501.

The most comprehensive exploration of cannibalism in the Pacific Northwest has been conducted by Jim McDowell in *Hamatsa: The Enigma of Cannibalism on the Pacific Northwest Coast* (Ronsdale, 1997). He traces the subject back to Florentine merchant-navigator Amerigo Vespucci who reached the continent named after him in 1501. "I spoke with a man who told me he had eaten 300 men," wrote Vespucci. He also reported seeing a sailor, sent ashore to charm or solicit some native women, attacked and eaten by them as his shipmates watched.

BOOKS: Edited by F.W. Howay for the Champlain Society in 1940, *The Journals of Captain James Colnett Aboard the Argonaut from April 26, 1789 to November 3, 1791* includes "A translation of the Diary of Esteban José Martínez from July 2 till July 14, 1789"; *Diary of the Voyage, in command of the frigate Princesa and the packet San Carlos in the present year of 1789* by Martínez was translated by William L. Schurz in 1900. A copy is in the University of B.C.'s Special Collections.

ANDREW BRACEY TAYLOR

"...nothing can appear more wretched than a Hut containing a Nutka family." —ANDREW BRACEY TAYLOR

One of the most obscure documents pertaining to fur trading on the B.C. coast in the 18th century is the journal of Andrew Bracey Taylor, third mate on the *Prince of Wales* during William Colnett's voyage to the Northwest Coast in 1786 to 1788.

As the only member of the expedition, other than Colnett, who held a commission in the Royal Navy, Taylor maintained a separate journal that now serves as a slightly more literate counterpoint to official records kept by Colnett. Taylor's account was presented in Robert M. Galois' *A Voyage to the North West Side of America: The Journals of James Colnett, 1786–89.*

"Taylor was also more aware of, or paid more attention to, the world of the seamen," Galois wrote. "Although shaped by the paternalism of command, and embodying the distinctions of class, his comments were closer to empathy than condescension." Galois has provided frequent samples of Taylor's hitherto unpublished journal, including the long poem of expectation that Taylor wrote about their journey to "Albions Coast." Upon their arrival at Nootka Sound, Taylor described the visit of the first canoes and several "troublesome elderly Men," one of whom was "a sourly fellow" who stood up and "harangued the Natives along side for near an hour without ceasing." After some afternoon trading for "Otter and other skins," Taylor described how many of the crew, extremely ill with scurvy, went ashore and fortified themselves with fresh air and the collecting of "a Vegetable similar to Spinach, known by the Name of fat hen!" Possibly writing with an eye towards eventual publication, Taylor records matters beyond his personal welfare.

"This evening I was Eye witness to the humanity of one of the Natives in assisting the sick over the Rocks into our Boat. He was an Elderly man and Father of a Family who had his house and occupied a small spot close to the Ship, his business was to attend the weakest of the Seamen one after the other, with great care and fellow feeling using all the tenderness and concern of a Brother or a Father to such as were able to walk without Aid. I rewarded his humanity in the best manner I was able. During my evening ramble He and his family requested me to fire a Pistol, and afterwards with permission fired one himself with great timidity & not without causing general fear for his safety throughout his Family. His Hut was filthy in extreme and everything within it, nothing can appear more wretched than a Hut containing a Nutka family. They offered me Fish, which was boiling at a wood fire, and were quite civil to all the Seamen."

During their stay at "Barclay's Cove," another name for Friendly Cove or Yuquot, Taylor observed the superiority of "Maquilla" [Maquinna] who "speaks some English, and is very ready in learning he has a very good notion of singing after the English manner." He also credits the preceding visit of Captain Barclay [Barkley] for establishing civil relations with the people of "Maquillas Village."

The *Prince of Wales* proceeded to the "Charlotte Isles" and onto Alaskan waters prior to wintering in Hawaii. It returned to the B.C. coast in 1788, reaching Macao to sell its accumulation of furs on November 11, 1788. The crew proceeded to Canton before the *Prince of Wales* returned to London with Taylor aboard and without Captain Colnett in charge. Overqualified for the position he held aboard the *Prince of Wales*, Taylor was sometimes critical of both Captain Colnett and Captain Duncan of the *Princess Royal*, both of whom had embarked from London in late September of 1786 for their two-vessel commercial enterprise on behalf of Richard Cadman Etches & Co.

Andrew Taylor was born sometime in the 1760s, into a naval family, and served at a young age during the American War of

Independence and during the siege of Gibraltar, then later in the West Indies. After the *Prince of Wales* reached Canton, he was appointed second mate for the final leg back to London. He was married in his hometown of Great Yarmouth on September 22, 1789. He continued to rise in rank during a varied naval career, including stints carrying British mail and passengers to Holland and the West Indies. He was briefly captured by a French privateer in March of 1799 but soon returned to service at St. Kitts in May. He died in Port Royal, Jamaica in January of 1800.

BOOKS: *A Voyage to the North West Side of America: The Journals of James Colnett, 1786–89*, ed. Robert Galois (Vancouver: UBC Press, 2004); James Colnett, *A Voyage to the South Atlantic and Round Cape Horn into the Pacific Ocean* (London: A. Arrowsmith et al, 1798; Amsterdam: N. Israel, 1968).

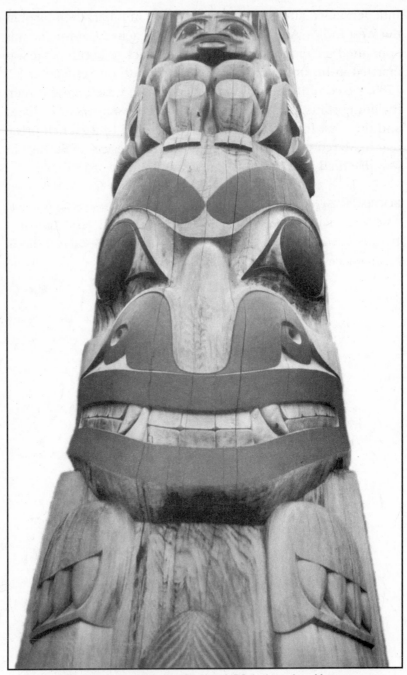

Haida totem pole carved by Jim Hart, UBC Anthropology Museum.

VI
AMERICANS

Robert Gray
Joseph Ingraham
Robert Haswell
John Bartlett
Ebenezer Johnson
John Boit
Charles Bishop

ROBERT GRAY

The first American to circumnavigate the globe, Robert Gray, played a significant role in the naming of British Columbia. The name is *not* directly derivative of Christopher Columbus.

Captain Gray ascended the mouth of the Columbia River in Oregon on May 11, 1792, naming the waterway after his ship the *Columbia Rediva* on May 18, 1792.

Five months later, as directed by Captain George Vancouver, Lieutenant William Broughton aboard the *Chatham* sent two smaller boats up the Columbia River for 100 miles, making a map that would be copied by the British mapmaker Aaron Arrowsmith. Captain Vancouver then arranged for Broughton, as his ranking subordinate, to travel across New Mexico, as sanctioned by his friend Captain Bodega y Quadra, in order to take a ship to England and report on his recent meetings with Quadra at Nootka Sound. Broughton arrived in England in July of 1793.

The subsequent designation of the name Columbia for the main fur trading river and the main fur trading region became useful when England needed to supply a name for territories it wished to secure north of the 49th parallel in keeping with a new bilateral treaty. Queen Victoria was given various options from which to choose for the naming of "North Columbia." New Cornwall was rejected, as was New Caledonia. She chose British Columbia.

Ironically, this designation can be traced to an American. Robert Gray's ship was named to honour St. Columb, one of the three patron saints of Ireland. (The orbiting space ship *Columbia* was also named by the U.S. space program in honour of Robert Gray's ship.)

Born in Tiverton, Rhode Island, in 1755, Gray is generally regarded as the first American to fly the Stars and Stripes of the 13 amalgamated colonies in the Pacific Northwest—although there are obscure claims that a New York brig called the *Eleanora,* commanded by Simon Metcalfe, might have preceded him. Gray has also been credited, rightly or wrongly, with the discovery of the Columbia River.

Having served in the navy during the American Revolution, probably as a privateer, Gray, along with Captain John Kendrick, born in Massachusetts around 1740, was hired by Boston merchants in August of 1787 to explore the northwest coast of North America and to open a fur trade with China on behalf of New England. The merchants were likely encouraged to do so by John Ledyard, who had sailed to the Pacific Northwest with Captain Cook.

With the onset of an economic depression in New England, largely due to the cessation of war, New Englanders

Robert Gray

were seeking new markets by sea, having developed a substantial merchant navy in order to fight the British. In 1784 the *Empress of China,* commanded by John Green, had reached Macao from New York after a six-month journey via the Cape of Good Hope, reaping a $30,000 profit from sales of wine, brandy, tar and turpentine. Hence the "Bostonians" made their first incursions into British Columbia.

Gray and Kendrick sailed two vessels, the 212-ton *Columbia Rediviva* and the 90-ton sloop *Lady Washington,* to the Falkland Islands via the Cape Verde Islands, parting company as they rounded Cape Horn and entered the Pacific. Gray's Black manservant was killed by Indians near Tillamook Bay, about 30 miles south of the as-yet unseen Columbia River mouth, whereupon Gray called the place Murderer's Harbor. This incident contributed to his subsequent distrustful relations with the Indians at Clayoquot.

Gray proceeded to Barkley Sound, then onto Clayoquot Sound—which they called Hancock Harbor—where third mate Robert Haswell, age nineteen, recorded their attempts to trade: "The principle or superior chief of this tribe's name is Wickananish he visated us accompaneyed by one of his brothers completely dressed in a genteerl sute of cloths which he said Capt Mears had given him, Capt. Mears name was not the only one they mentioned for they spoke of Capt. Barkley Capt Hannah Capt Dunkin and Capt Duglas what they said of them we now knew so little of there language we could not comprehend."

As recorded by trader John Meares, Gray arrived at Nootka in command of the *Lady Washington* on September 17, 1788. He and John Kendrick were the harbingers of "American free enterprise" in British Columbia. Ultimately Americans would break the monopoly of the East India Company and become dominant in the Northwest fur trade. Upon his arrival, Meares tried dissuading the Americans from trading.

Robert Haswell was not deceived by Meares. "All the time these gentlemen were on board they fully employed themselves falsicating and rehursing vague and improvable tales relative to the coast of the vast danger attending its nagivation of the monsterous savage disposition of its inhabitants adding it would be maddness in us so week as we were to stay a winter among them.... The fact was they wished to frighten us off the coast that they alone might menopolise the trade but the debth of there design could be easily fathemed."

Captain Kendrick arrived at Nootka in the *Columbia*, having lost two of his crewmen to scurvy. Captain Gray assisted Meares in repairing his ships so that by early fall the *Felice*, the *Iphigenia* and the newly built *North West America* all left Friendly Cove to winter in Hawaii.

Gray and his cohort Kendrick exchanged ships in 1789.

Taking charge of the *Columbia*, Gray took a cargo of sea otter skins to Guangzhou, but met with limited success. He sailed westward until he reached Boston in 1790, thereby completing the first American circumnavigation of the globe.

On September 28, 1790, Gray sailed from Boston on a second expedition to the Pacific Northwest, wintering over and arriving at Clayoquot, the American trading fort on Vancouver Island, on June 5, 1791. Sailing as far north as Portland Channel, some of Gray's men on the *Columbia* were killed by Indians. Kendrick also made a return voyage, reaching the Queen Charlotte Islands where he and the crew of the *Lady Washington* were attacked and Kendrick's son was killed. Both ships returned to Clayoquot. Kendrick left for China with his furs. He would later die in Hawaii from injuries suffered from a gun explosion.

Gray wintered with much difficulty at an encampment on Meares Island called Fort Defiance, where he built a sloop called the *Adventure.*

The Indians at Clayoquot were far from friendly. Suspecting a plot against him, Gray took pre-emptive action and burned their village at Opitsat. The *Columbia* and the *Adventure* left Clayoquot on April 2, 1792. The *Adventure* was sent north to trade for furs while Gray and the *Columbia* sailed south. During this voyage he lay for nine days off the mouth of a large river, but did not attempt entry.

Returning north, Gray met Captain George Vancouver on April 28, 1792, and exchanged information with him, including a mention of this large river. Captain Vancouver was skeptical and wrote in his journal at the time, "If any river should be found, it must be a very intricate one and inaccessible to vessels of our burden."

Gray headed south once more, reaching Gray's Harbour on the coast of Washington State. (He called it Bulfinch Harbour after one of his sponsors, but Captain Vancouver renamed it Gray's Harbour.) Gray reached Cape Disappointment on the Oregon coast and once more found the mouth of the great river. On May 7, 1792, he wrote: "Being within six miles of the land, saw an entrance in the same, which had a very good appearance of a harbor.... We soon saw from our masthead a passage in between the sand-bars. At half past three, bore away, and ran in north-east by east, having from four to eight fathoms, sandy bottom; and as we drew in nearer between the bars, had from ten to thirteen fathoms, having a very strong tide of ebb to stem.... At five P.M. came to in five fathoms water, sandy bottom, in a safe harbor, well sheltered from the sea by long sand-bars and spits."

Gray ascended the Columbia River on May 11, 1792, naming the waterway after his ship on May 18, 1792. Later the Columbia River would be used as the main interior waterway for the fur trade in the western U.S. but in 1792 Gray described what he saw without much enthusiasm. After his explorations of the Pacific Northwest, Gray sold furs in China in 1793 and returned to a career of sailing on the east coast of the United States. He died poverty-stricken in Charleston in 1806.

BOOKS: John Scofield, *Hail, Columbia: Robert Gray, John Kendrick and the Pacific Fur Trade* (Portland: Oregon Historical Society Press, 1993).

JOSEPH INGRAHAM

"...an intelligent fellow of considerable talent and great experience on the coast." —CAPTAIN BODEGA Y QUADRA'S ESTIMATION OF INGRAHAM

One of the crewmen for Robert Gray's completion of the first American circumnavigation of the globe in 1790 was Joseph Ingraham, who served as second mate on the *Columbia* in 1789.

Sometime during the first half of that year Ingraham provided an undated letter to Esteban José Martínez at Nootka to corroborate that he believed the first ship to visit Nootka Sound was Spanish: "our stay here enabled us to converse so well with the natives as to put beyond a doubt [that] there was one ship here before

A drawing by Joseph Ingraham, 1792.

him [Cook], and this they inadvertently inform'd us of their own accord." Ingraham went so far as to reiterate the Spanish claim that two silver spoons purchased by one of Captain Cook's men at Nootka Sound could only have originated from that preceding Spanish ship. This self-serving cooperation of an American to gain an advantage over their British competition might have accounted for Quadra's gracious estimation of Ingraham's character.

A Boston merchant hired Ingraham to sail from 1790 to 1792 to the Pacific Northwest to bring back furs in the brigantine *Hope*. He visited the Queen Charlotte Islands in July of 1791 and sailed for China in August, hoping to sell his cache, but was stymied by fractious relations between the Chinese and the Russians at the time.

Ingraham returned the following summer and amicably met Captain Bodega y Quadra at Nootka Sound in July of 1792. Ingraham later met Robert Gray in the Queen Charlotte Islands on July 23, 1792. He sailed back to Boston, having failed commercially.

Ingraham made some maps and kept a journal. One of his maps identifies Vancouver Island simply as Quadra's Isle. Later Captain Quadra met Captain Vancouver in Nootka Sound and agreed the island should be called "Quadra and Vancouver's Island." A copy of Ingraham's *Hope* journal became significant in the 1830s when American historian Robert Greenhow tried to substantiate American claims to the Oregon Territory.

BOOKS: *Journal of the Brigantine Hope on a Voyage to the Northwest Coast of North America 1790–92*, ed. M.A. Barre (Kaplanoff Imprint Society, 1971). Original in Library of Congress, Washington, D.C.

━━━━❈❈❈━━━━

ROBERT HASWELL

American trade in the Pacific began when Robert Morris sent the *Empress of China* to trade with the Orient in 1784. Three years later Joseph Barrel initiated a three-way system of commerce with the *Lady Washington*: American goods from the eastern seaboard were traded to the Indians in exchange for furs; these furs were sold in Canton; and profits were used to purchase textiles, porcelain, tea and other items from the Orient.

When Robert Gray returned to Clayoquot in September of 1791, he constructed a fort and also built a sloop called the *Adventure*. He placed it under the command of Robert Haswell, his second officer, born on November 24, 1768, probably in Nantasket, Massachusetts. The memoirs of Haswell and his fellow crewmembers John Boit and John Hoskins were not published during their lifetimes.

As trade in Alaska became more problematic due to violence and competition, Robert Gray's discovery of the Columbia River led sailors such as Haswell and Boit to speculate in their diaries about the possibilities of increased trade in the Columbia River region, giving rise to Astoria and the Oregon Territory dispute.

Whereas "King George Men"—as the Indians called them—were concerned with politics as well as commerce, the "Boston

Men"—as the Americans were known—were exclusively interested in commerce. This proved advantageous for the Americans. As neutrals, they could play one side against the other and simultaneously remain aloof from the geopolitical rivalries between the Spanish and British.

As recorded by Haswell, relations between Americans and the British were soured by the deceitful efforts of John Meares who tried unsuccessfully to mislead American traders in 1788. Conversely, relations between Americans and the Spanish were enhanced by a firm friendship between John Kendrick and Nootka commander Martínez who first met on May 6, 1789 (while Kendrick was repairing the *Columbia* inside Nootka Sound).

Robert Haswell, lost at sea.

John Kendrick was influential in his relations with the Nuu-chah-nulth. Moziña records that Kendrick "for ten guns and a little powder, bought a piece of land in Maquinnas on which to spend the winter. He gained the friendship of the natives as no one else had, continually giving them presents, entertaining them with fireworks, speaking their language, wearing their clothes, and, in a word, adapting himself to all their customs. I cannot say whether it was self-interest or rivalry with the English that suggested to the Americans the perverse idea of teaching the savages the handling of firearms—a lesson that could be harmful to all humanity. He [Kendrick] gave Maquinna a swivel gun; he furnished Wickinanish with more than two hundred guns, two barrels of powder, and a considerable portion of shot, which [the Indians] have just finished using on the unhappy sailors of Captains Brown and Baker."

The little-known logs of Haswell, Boit and Hoskins were first published in 1941 within a composite volume edited by F.W. Howay. Haswell's journal is *A Voyage Around the World on Board the Ship Columbia Rediviva and Sloop Washington in 1787–89*. After Haswell wrote to his half-sister saying his profession had "impaired my constitution beyond measure," he married in 1798 and joined the navy in 1799. Leaving the navy at age thirty-two, he took command of the *Louisa*, sailed from Boston in 1801 for the Pacific Northwest, and was lost at sea with his crew.

BOOKS: *Voyages of the Columbia to the Northwest Coast, 1787–90 and 1790–93*, ed. F.W. Howay (Massachusetts Historical Society Collections, Vol. LXXIX, Cambridge, Massachusetts: Harvard University Press, 1941); *Robert Haswell's Log of the First Voyage of the "Columbia" [1787–1789]*, pp. 3-107 in *Voyages of the "Columbia" to the Northwest Coast, 1787–1790 and 1790–1793*, ed. F.W. Howay (New York: Da Capo Press, 1969).

JOHN BARTLETT

American sailor John Bartlett's journal description of a 45-ft. high Haida totem pole on Langara Island in 1791 has been cited as the earliest literary evidence of a totem pole "known to science." According to Robin K. Wright, John Bartlett also made the first drawing of a carved house frontal pole on the Northwest Coast in the Haida village of Dadens on Langara or North Island in 1791. The following year Etienne Marchand provided the first detailed description of a Haida heraldic pole erected in front of a house as an entranceway.

In July of 1791, Malaspina's artist, José Cardero, sketched a Tlingit mortuary crest suspended between two poles at Mulgrave, Alaska, now known as Yakutat Bay, and discovered it was the grave of a woman. He also sketched several pyres and a grave overseen by a "colossal monster" carving made of "pine" (Sitka spruce).

This is the first known drawing of a totem pole in the Queen Charlotte Islands. It was sketched by John Bartlett in 1791. It shows a frontal pole about 40 feet high in the village of Dadens on Langara Island where Juan Pérez had made the first European contact in 1774. Bartlett wrote in his journal, "The Dore of it is made like a man['s] head the Passage in to the House is in Between his teath and was Boult be fore thay nkowd the youse of Iron."

John Webber's earlier sketches of carved interior house pillars at Nootka Sound in 1778 were published in Cook's journal in 1784.

Bartlett was a common sailor aboard the British ship *Mercury*, owned and commanded by John Henry Cox, when it sailed from England. Once the ship reached the Pacific its name was changed to *Gustavus III*, and the crew sailed under a Swedish flag. Bartlett visited Unalaska in October and November of 1789. Bartlett Cove and Gustavus are two tiny outposts ten miles apart within Glacier Bay National Park in Alaska.

According to F.W. Howay, *Gustavus III* also lay at anchor at Clayoquot for about ten days in March of 1791. The crew traded on the coast from March until July, with Thomas Barnett serving as master.

BOOKS: John Bartlett's journal of the *Gustavus*, 1791, appears within *A Narrative of Events in the Life of John Bartlett of Boston, Massachusetts, in the Years 1790–1793, During Voyages to Canton, the Northwest Coast of North America, and Elsewhere*, pp. 287-343, which is again within *The Sea, the Ship, and the Sailor: Tales of Adventure from Log Books and Original Narratives, By Charles H. Barnard, John Nicol, John B. Knights, William Mariner, John Bartlett* edited by Elliot Snow (Salem, Massachusetts: Marine Research Society, 1925).

<hr>

EBENEZER JOHNSON

"Distressing is our situation on account of bad provisions by the neglect of the owners of the Ship, confined to three small biscuits per day, and three pints of water. In this situation for three months, with a small allowance of beef." —EBENEZER JOHNSON

Of all 18th-century journals pertaining in some way to British Columbia, Ebenezer Johnson's tale is the most humble, and also one of the rarest. Although many American seamen came to the North Pacific on dozens of American ships, and several kept journals, no other accounts of maritime fur trading were published in their lifetimes.

In 1974, university librarian Basil Stuart-Stubbs selected Johnson's diary for republication in 450 copies by the Alcuin Society of Vancouver. Precious few 18th-century copies are known to exist: one is at the Houghton Library in Harvard, another belongs to the American Antiquarian Society and a third is stored at UBC Special Collections. "Johnson's Short Account," according to Stuart-Stubbs, "seems to be the sole example of a contemporarily published personal narrative arising from an American voyage in this period. It appeared in Massachusetts in 1798, the same year in which Vancouver's account was printed in London."

(The journal of seventeen-year-old American William Sturgis' 1799 visit to the coast on the *Eliza* was edited by S.W. Jackman and published by Sono Nis Press in 1978. See Addenda.)

Johnson was a common sailor, a young man with limited education, who endured scurvy on the *India Packet*, captained by William Rogers from August 29, 1796 to April 10, 1798. Built in Braintree, Massachusetts in 1795 and owned by Dorr and Sons of Boston, the *India Packet* was a three-masted, square-sterned ship with two decks, only 88 feet long and 24 feet wide, 12 feet deep and weighing 226 tons. Johnson spent a year-and-a-half at sea and managed only about 1,000 words in his diary, plus a concluding original poem that expresses his relief at returning safely ("Blest with Neptune smiles we fly"). Friends apparently encouraged him to self-publish his 15-page memoir in 1798.

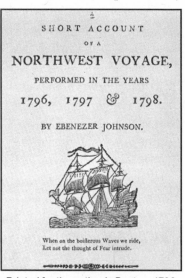

A
SHORT ACCOUNT
OF A
NORTHWEST VOYAGE,
PERFORMED IN THE YEARS
1796, 1797 & 1798.
BY EBENEZER JOHNSON.

When on the boisterous Waves we ride,
Let not the thought of Fear intrude.

Printed for the author in Boston, 1798.

Johnson's ship reached the Queen Charlotte Islands in February of 1797. He provides some cursory descriptions of meeting Indians at "Charlotte's Island" but their trade was initially limited due to "boisterous weather." He writes, "We then thought best to sail for Skiticus [Skidegate] still further to the Southward, the distance about 40 miles. After arriving, we came to anchor, and find here a large Village rather a metropolis of this Nation, where we purchased three hundred skins."

BOOKS: *A Short Account of a Northwest Voyage, Performed in the Years 1796, 1797 & 1798*, ed. M.S. Batts, with an introduction by Basil Stuart-Stubbs, illustrations by Fritz Jacobsen (Vancouver: Alcuin Society, 1974).

JOHN BOIT

"The females was not very chaste, but their lip pieces was enough to disgust any civilized being. However some of the Crew was quite partial." —JOHN BOIT, AGE SIXTEEN

Born in Boston on October 15, 1774, John Boit served on the *Columbia Rediviva*'s second voyage to the West Coast of America and China from 1790 to 1793. He described Nootka Sound as a sixteen-year-old, making him one of the youngest of the 18th-century chroniclers of British Columbia.

In the spring of 1792, the *Columbia* reached land between Nootka Sound and Clayoquot Sound, where Boit observed:

"Hannah, Chief of the Ahhousett came on board and appeared friendly. Above 300 of the Natives was alongside in the course of the day. Their canoes was made from the body of a tree, with stem and stern pieces neatly fixed on. Their models was not unlike our Nantucket whale boats. The dress of these Indians was either the Skin of some Animal, or else a Blankett of their own manufactory, made of some kind of Hair. This garment was slung over the right shoulder. They all appear'd very friendly, brought us plenty of fish and greens. We tarry'd in this harbour till the 16th [of] June; [we] landed our sick immediately on our arrival and pitch'd a tent for their reception, and although there was ten of them in the last stage of Scurvy, still they soon recover'd, upon smelling the turf and eating greens of various kinds. We buried severall of our sick up to the Hips in the earth, and let them remain for hours in that situation. We found this method of great service. The principall village in this harbour is called Opitsatah, and is governed by Wickananish, a warlike Chief. He and his family visited us often. The Indians brought severall Deer, and plenty of Rock Cod, Salmon, and other fish. Wild parsley, and a root call'd Isau or Isop by the natives and much resembling a small onion, was brought us in abundance. We purchas'd many of the Sea Otter skins in exchange for Copper, and blue Cloth. These Indians are of a large size, and somewhat corpulent. The Men wear no other covering but the garment before mentioned, and seem to have no sense of shame, as they appear in a state of Nature. The Women stand in great fear of the Males, but appear to be naturally very modest. Their garment is manufactured from the bark of a tree and is well executed, being so constructed as to cover them complete from the Neck to the Ancle. Both Male and Female wear Hats of a conicle form made out of strong reeds. On them is painted (in a rude manner) their mode of Whale fishery. Attoo, the Captain's servant (and a native of the Sandwich Isle [Hawaii]), ran away among the Indians. A chief coming on board, [we] plac'd a guard over him, and sent his Canoe back to the village with the news. They [the Indians] soon return'd with Mr. Attoo, and ransom'd their Chief."

The *Columbia* under Captain Robert Gray left Cox's Harbour with the crew rejuvenated by spruce tea. They sailed northwest to a cove they named Columbias where "vast many natives" came alongside. They laid up in the harbour until June 26, acquiring furs in exchange for copper, iron and cloth. They also traded small items for fish, greens and a few deer.

Like the Indians at Clayoquot, according to Boit, the Indians at Nootka Sound would "pilfer whenever an opportunity offer'd. Their Women were more Chaste than those we had lately left. But still they were not all Dianas." [Diana was a Roman goddess identified with the Greek Artemis, honoured for her virginity.]

Boit visited one of the villages where he watched Indians making canoes and drying fish. On June 28 the *Columbia* entered the Strait of Juan de Fuca "abreast the Village of Nittenatt" where "[it] was evident that these Natives had been visited by that scourge of mankind—the Smallpox. The Spaniards, as the natives say, brought it among them. These Indians appear'd friendly."

The expedition reached "a small Isle call'd Tatooch" [Tatoosh

Based on a sketch by Capt. George Dixon, this labreted Haida woman was drawn by an unknown artist in 1787. A breast was exposed to ensure she was identifiable as female.

Island] where the local chief offered to sell some young children captured in warfare.

Boit reached Houston Stewart Channel on the southeast portion of the Queen Charlotte Islands on July 8, 1791. The expedition was met by a chief called Coyac.

Of the Haida, Boit observed, "The Women are entirely cover'd with Garments of their own manufactory from the bark of trees. They appear to carry full sway over the men and have an incision cut through the under lip, which they spread out with a piece of wood, about the size and shape of a goose egg (some much larger). It's considered as an ornament, but in my opinion looks very gastly. Some of them booms out two inches from the chin. The women appear very fond of their offspring, and the Men of both.

"We remain'd in this sound till the 17th. During which time we purchas'd a good lot of Sea Otter and other furs chiefly for Iron and Cloth. Copper was not in demand. The boats were sent frequently after wood and water, but were always well arm'd. The Natives supplied us with plenty of Halibut and Rock Cod, for which we paid them in Nails. Wild fowl was plenty in this Sound, of which we caught and kill'd many. I landed at one of their villages, found the Indians comfortably lodg'd, and [they] kept large fires although the weather was temperate. When I went into one of their houses they was eating coast muscles and singing a warlike Song. They appear'd fond of our visit and never molested any thing in the boat. Their canoes are not made near so neat as those we had seen before, but I think they was more commodious. The females was not very chaste, but their lip pieces was enough to disgust any civilized being. However some of the Crew was quite partial."

At age nineteen, John Boit was appointed to serve as a merchant sea captain on the *Union* that embarked from Newport, Rhode Island, in August of 1794. In an era when most sailors could not expect to live beyond age thirty, and British subjects could become midshipmen in Her Majesty's Navy at age ten, Boit's teenage captaincy was not remarkable.

For his return trip to North America he sailed via the Cape Verde and Falkland Islands, reaching Vancouver Island on May 16, 1795. He gathered sea otter pelts from the Columbia River to Dixon Entrance. He intended to winter in Hawaii until an Eng-

lishman who was serving as an advisor to King Kamehameha warned Boit that his ship might be seized by the Hawaiians. The *Union* sailed the next day and reached China by the end of November where Boit sold his cargo of 150 sea otter pelts, 300 beaver pelts and other land furs.

By mid-March, Boit reached Mauritius (Isle de France). He arrived in Boston on July 8, 1796. In doing so, he earned his reputation in maritime history by being the first American to circumnavigate the globe in a sloop and not lose a man in the process.

In the Strait of Juan de Fuca, Chief Tetacu offered to sell children captured in warfare to John Boit near "a small Isle call'd Tatooch" [Tatoosh Island]. Drawing by José Cardero.

Half-owned by Boit's brother-in-law, the *Union* was a 65-ft., 94-ton topsail sloop with a crew of 22, heavily armed with cannon. Boit declared the *Union* was "an excellent sea boat...a very safe vessel, still I think it too great a risque for to trust to one mast on such a long voyage." Boit's republished log is illustrated with detailed drawings of the *Union* by Hewitt Jackson. Boit remained a sea captain until his death at age fifty-five in 1829.

BOOKS: *A New Log of the Columbia, 1790–1792*, ed. Edmund S. Meany (Seattle: University of Washington Press, 1921); *The Log of the Union: John Boit's Remarkable Voyage to the Northwest Coast and Around the World, 1794–1796*, ed. Edmund Hayes (Portland: Western Imprints, The Press of the Oregon Historical Society, 1981).

CHARLES BISHOP

Charles Bishop sailed on the *Ruby* from Bristol in 1794 to conduct trade for sea otter furs on the northwest coast of America alongside the *Nautilus*. Bishop was an employee of the Bristol ship builder Sydenham Teast.

In 1795, the *Ruby* returned to winter for three months in "Deception [Baker] Bay" among the Chinook Indians. Bishop wrote, "Their Former disposition to thieving is much abated. We have lost nothing, but when any of the inferiour people contrived to perloin a Knife or any article, upon aquainting the chiefs we generally have had it restored the next day. One of the Rubys People stole an Arrow, and upon its being Discovered, he was tied up and got a severe Flogging, this and several other circumstances has given these people great confidance in us. A trifling Present now and then gratifies their Desires, and which is generally returned by a Present of Fish or Cran-berries, nor do they withhold their Daughters, some of whom are well Featured young Women."

In the southern hemisphere Bishop was one of the first sealers to operate around the Furneaux Islands near Tasmania. He established the first settlement south of Sydney.

BOOKS: *The Journal and Letters of Captain Charles Bishop on the Northwest Coast of America, in the Pacific and in New South Wales 1794–1802*, ed. Michael Roe (Cambridge: Hakluyt Society, 1967).

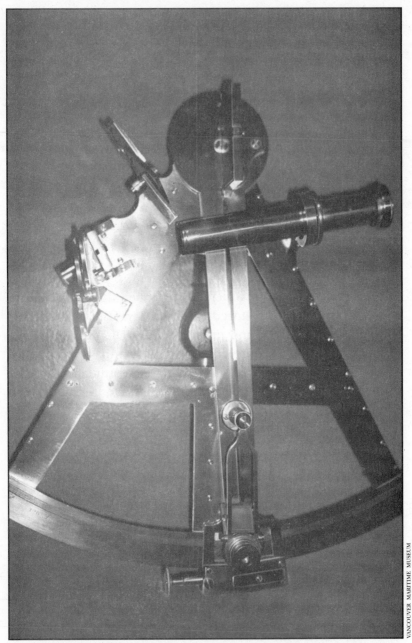

This sextant was used by Joseph Baker—after whom Mount Baker is named—for his survey work with Captain George Vancouver's expedition to the Pacific Northwest. It is on display at the Vancouver Maritime Museum.

VII
MAPMAKERS

George Vancouver
Archibald Menzies
William Broughton
Edward Bell
Alexander Mackenzie

GEORGE VANCOUVER

"I cannot possibly believe that any uncultivated country had ever been discovered exhibiting so rich a picture." —GEORGE VANCOUVER

Captain George Vancouver conducted the longest survey voyage in the world's history but he remains the second-most renowned mariner of the Pacific Northwest—after his mentor Captain Cook.

Born of Dutch stock in King's Lynn, Norfolk, England on June 22, 1757, George Vancouver entered the British Navy in 1771 and first sailed under Captain James Cook upon turning fifteen. He accompanied Cook on his second and third voyages from Antarctica to Alaska. Vancouver was badly beaten by Hawaiians the day before Cook was killed.

Promoted to lieutenant in 1780, Vancouver fought against the French in the West Indies and received orders in December of 1790 to prepare to sail to Nootka to resolve territorial conflicts with Spain and to survey the coast from California to Alaska. Vancouver set sail from England as captain of the *Discovery* in 1791. In April he passed through the Strait of Juan de Fuca, surveying the mainland coast and reaching the site of the city that bears his name.

In June of 1792, he met two Spanish vessels off Point Grey in Vancouver harbour, giving rise to the name Spanish Banks. The Spanish captains were Galiano and Cayetano Valdés. Vancouver then sailed to Nootka Sound in August and famously met and befriended the commander Bodega y Quadra. He and Quadra couldn't agree upon what area was to be ceded to Britain in keeping with the Nootka Convention, but they agreed to call Vancouver Island "the Island of Quadra and Vancouver." This name appeared on early admiralty maps until Hudson's Bay Company traders abbreviated the name to "Vancouver's Island."

Vancouver continued his meticulous surveys of the West Coast in the summers of 1793 and 1794, wintering in Hawaii. He is commonly credited as being the first mariner to circumnavigate Vancouver Island when in fact he was the first European to prove it was an island with his various surveys.

Nine Spanish maps were provided to George Vancouver after he arrived on the coast in the summer of 1792, including charts made by Alejandro Malaspina while anchored at Nootka.

In 1792 an excellent map of southwestern B.C. waters was made by Dionisio Alcalá Galiano (the first European to find the mouth of the Fraser River) but Britain published Vancouver's charts four years before Spain released Galiano's charts in 1802.

George Vancouver's work was not flawless. He missed the mouths of the Fraser, Skeena and Stikine Rivers, and he overlooked Seymour Inlet

This well-known portrait has never been positively identified as Captain George Vancouver.

opposite the north end of Vancouver Island.

Vancouver provided the permanent names for many places along the coast, as well as some toponyms that did not stick. For instance, he named northern Washington as New Georgia, and successive northerly regions as New Hanover, New Cornwall and New Norfolk. Other locations were named for his officers Zachary Mudge, Peter Puget, Joseph Baker, Joseph Whidbey, William Broughton and James Johnstone. The 297-ton *Discovery* returned to England in October of 1795.

Vancouver did not discover Vancouver Harbour. This modernist anchor by artist Christel Fuoss-Moore, erected at Spanish Banks during the Vancouver Centennial in 1986, marks the arrival of Spanish explorer Don José Maria Narváez on July 5, 1791.

In the wake of Vancouver's remarkably accurate survey work, competing British and Spanish sea captains gave up the quest for the Northwest Passage. A sea route connecting the two oceans was eventually found by Norwegian Roald Amundsen when he sailed from Oslo with six others in the 47-ton sloop *Gjöa* in 1903 and reached Nome, Alaska on August 31, 1906.

George Vancouver's downfall was his flogging of sixteen-year-old Thomas Pitt, an obnoxious member of the leading political family in Britain. Having been a shipmate with Captain Bligh on Captain James Cook's third voyage, Vancouver was later counselled by Bligh not to spare the rod on his crew following the infamous "mutiny on the Bounty." Vancouver, a stern disciplinarian, was within his rights to order a third flogging of

Pitt, who was strongly suspected of thievery, but Vancouver was never vindicated in his lifetime.

After Vancouver sent Pitt home in disgrace on the supply ship *Daedalus* in 1794, Pitt maligned Vancouver in upper-class society. When Pitt later became 2nd Baron of Camelford, he challenged Vancouver to a duel. Already ailing, Vancouver would not oblige him, whereupon Pitt attacked him in the street, leading to a front-page scandal.

Vancouver had trouble collecting his back pay and his achievements were never adequately recognized. He spent his declining years in ill health, preparing his journals for publication with the aid of his brother John. Shortly after George Vancouver's death at age forty on May 10, 1798, his adventures were published and proved extremely popular.

A Voyage of Discovery to the North Pacific Ocean and Round the World is one of the first books to describe the B.C. coast at length. A first edition set of the original three-volume *Voyage of Discovery*, valued at $25,000, was purchased and donated to the Vancouver Maritime Museum by Alcan in 1997. The National Library of Canada also retains a copy.

In 1999, the Friends of George Vancouver Society initiated a proclamation signed by the Lieutenant Governor of British Columbia to formally exonerate Vancouver ("whereas his reputation has been unjustly maligned"). This proclamation declared that May 12, the date of Vancouver's death, would be George Vancouver Day in British Columbia in perpetuity.

It is seldom noted that Spanish pilot José Maria Narváez preceded Vancouver to the entrance to English Bay within the Canadian city that now bears Vancouver's name.

BOOKS: *A Voyage of Discovery to the North Pacific Ocean [...] in Which the Coast of North-West America Has Been Carefully Examined and Accurately Surveyed [...] and Performed in the Years 1790, 1791, 1792, 1793, 1794, and 1795 [...].* (London: G.G. and J. Robinson, and J. Edwards, 1798); *A Voyage of Discovery to the North Pacific Ocean, 1791–1794,* ed. W. Kaye Lamb, 4 vols (London: Hakluyt Society, 1984).

ARCHIBALD MENZIES

Archibald Menzies, the lone civilian on Captain Vancouver's voyage, was one of the first British scientists to venture into the North Pacific. He is credited with taking the first Douglas fir (*Pseudotsuga menziesii*) specimen to England, as well as introducing the monkey puzzle tree to Europe. He also provided the scientific name for the arbutus tree (*Arbutus menziesii*) known in the United States as the madrona. It is the only broad-leafed evergreen tree native to Canada.

Menzies first collected West Coast specimens on the trading ship *Prince of Wales* commanded by Captain James Colnett in 1787 and 1788. For his return voyage with Vancouver, Menzies was able to have a twelve-by-eight-foot glass frame constructed on Vancouver's quarterdeck to house specimens—whether Vancouver wanted it there or not. Vancouver and Menzies were frequently at odds, partly because Menzies had been on the coast previously, at Nootka Sound. Menzies was also an appointee of Joseph Banks, the powerful President of the Royal Society who had sailed with Cook on his first voyage. Due to his somewhat lowly origins, Vancouver had to be wary of Banks' power and therefore he was less than welcoming to Menzies—the eyes and ears of Banks during the voyage.

In the spirit of Captain Cook's voyages, Archibald Menzies had been instructed to keep extensive notes about

Archibald Menzies was the chief scientist and frequent adversary of Captain Vancouver.

the natural history of each place, ascertaining whether plants cultivated in Europe were likely to thrive. He was also required to make ethnographic observations. Whereas Menzies' mandate was scientific, Vancouver's assigned tasks were geographic and diplomatic.

Archibald Menzies came from a family of botanists. He studied in Edinburgh and joined the Royal Navy as an assistant surgeon in 1782. After the voyage of the *Discovery* with Vancouver, Menzies served with the navy in the West Indies. He received a medical degree from Aberdeen University in 1799. Upon resigning from the navy in 1802, he practised medicine in Notting Hill, London.

Menzies was born on March 15, 1754 near Aberfeldy, Perthshire in Scotland. He died in London on February 15, 1842. His plant collection is displayed by London's Linnean Society, of which he was a member for more than 50 years. Menzies Bay north of Campbell River is presumed to be named in his honour.

BOOKS: Archibald Menzies, *Journal of Vancouver's Voyage, April to October, 1792*, ed. C.F. Newcombe (Victoria, B.C. Archives: Government of British Columbia, 1923); *The Alaska Travel Journals of Archibald Menzies, 1793–1794*, ed. Wallace Olson (University of Alaska Press, 1993).

WILLIAM BROUGHTON

Broughton Street in Vancouver, Broughton Island and Broughton Strait off Vancouver Island are named for William Robert Broughton, Captain Vancouver's second-in-command who captained the *HMS Chatham*. Broughton is important historically because Britain based its claim to the Oregon Territory largely on Broughton's explorations of the Columbia watershed. Broughton also first described Mt. Hood in Oregon.

Born in 1763 in Cheshire, England, he served as a midshipman in the American Revolutionary War in 1776 and sailed with Captain Knight on *HMS Victory* in 1790. After Vancouver completed negotiations with Bodega y Quadra at Nootka Sound, he sent Broughton back to Britain asking for further instructions.

In July of 1793, Broughton reached London where he was given command of *HMS Providence* in October. Broughton embarked from Plymouth in February of 1795, with Zachary Mudge as his second-in-command, but failed to reunite with Vancouver who had already reached the Atlantic on his return voyage.

Broughton reached Nootka Sound for the second time in March of 1796. He consulted with his officers and they decided—erroneously—that Captain Vancouver had probably already surveyed the west coast of South America as instructed. They set sail for Asia to survey the coast from Sakhalin to the Nanking River.

After Broughton crossed the Pacific to Korea and Japan, the *Providence* sank off Taiwan but Broughton had already taken the precautionary measure of obtaining a second ship in Macao, the *Prince William Henry*, with which he was able to complete his voyage back to Britain. He described his surveying expedition in a book that appeared in 1804.

Broughton was Commodore in the East Indies from 1807 to 1809, leading to his unsuccessful attack on Java and his return to Britain in 1812. He became Colonel of Marines in 1819 and died in Florence in 1821.

BOOKS: *A Voyage of Discovery in the North Pacific Ocean* (London: Cadell and Davies, 1804); *Voyage de découvertes dans la partie Septentrionale de l'Océan Pacifique, fait par le capitaine W. R. Broughton, commandant de la corvette de S.M.B. la Providence et sa conserve, pendant les années 1795, 1796, 1797 et 1798; dans lequel il a parcouru et visité la côte d'Asie, depuis le 35e degré nord, jusqu'au 52e; l'île d'Insu, ordinairement appelée Jesso; les côtes Nord, Est et Sud du Japon; les îles de Likeujo et autres îles voisines, ainsi que la côte de Corée. Traduit par ordre de S. E. le ministre de la marine et des colonies, par J. B. B. E*****, translated by Jean-Baptiste Benoît Eyriès (1807); *A Voyage of Discovery in the North Pacific Ocean* (Amsterdam: Biblioteca Australiana #13, 1967).

EDWARD BELL

"...the fleshy parts of his thighs were most butcherly cut out..."

Edward Bell was a crewman aboard the *Chatham* that accompanied Captain Vancouver's ship the *Discovery*, surveying the Pacific Northwest. In his diary Bell provided a circumstantial description of the murder of one of Captain Quadra's servants after his body was discovered naked and mutilated at Friendly Cove on September 14, 1792.

Edward Bell wrote in his diary, "A fine little Spanish boy—one of Mr. Quadra's servants, who had been missing about eight and forty hours—was found most barbarously murdered in a small bight within the Cove where the ships lay. A bloody knife was found lying near him. It is supposed he was decoyed thither by some of the Indians, under the pretence of gratifying an illicit intercourse with one of their women. But no reason could be assigned whatever for the taking away his life. No quarrel was known [to have] happened between the Indians and him or any of the Spaniards. On the contrary, the Indians enjoyed a happier time since the Spaniards had been first here. None of his clothes were to be found, but he was left naked with his throat cut from ear to ear. He had several stabs and cuts in his arms and on the backs of his hands, and the calves of his legs, and the fleshy parts of his thighs were most butcherly cut out and supposed to be eaten by the savage perpetrators of this act."

Bell's captain on the *Chatham* was Peter Puget, after whom Puget Sound is named.

BOOKS: *A New Vancouver Journal on the Discovery of Puget Sound, by [Edward Bell] a Member of Chatham's Crew* (Seattle: University of Washington, 1915).

ALEXANDER MACKENZIE

The most famous words in British Columbia history
were etched on a rock:

Alex Mackenzie
from Canada
by land
22nd July 1793.

Born in 1764 at Stornoway, Isle of Lewis, Scotland, Alexander Mackenzie came to the United States at age ten with his father. After his widowed father was killed in the Revolutionary War, he was sent to live with aunts in Montreal. He entered the employ of a nascent fur trading company, started by Gregory McLeod, that became part of the North West Company.

As a Nor'wester, Mackenzie was sent to the Athabasca River area where he first heard about a great river that might take him to the salt waters of the Pacific. It was referred to by his Indian informants as "the stinking lake."

In seeking that lake in 1789, Mackenzie accidentally became the first European to reach the mouth of the Arctic river that bears his name.

He resumed his quest to find a path across the continent in 1793 with nine men, one dog and one canoe. With the essential help of Indian guides, Mackenzie went up the Peace River, across the Rocky Mountains, part way down the Fraser River and traversed the Chilcotin on the oolichan "grease trail" used for trading among the First Nations. Reaching the mouth of the Bella Coola River on North Bentinck Arm, Mackenzie did not immediately record his presence on the Pacific.

Mackenzie and his men were upbraided by Bella Bella Indians who reported being recently fired upon by white men in a large canoe. It is known that one of the boats from Captain George Vancouver's *Discovery* had been in Dean Channel six weeks previously. Mackenzie recorded in his journal the names of two white men who were repeatedly referred to by the Indians as "Macubah" and "Benzins." They were likely referring to Captain Vancouver ["Macubah"] and botanist Archibald Menzies ["Benzins"]. Hence Mackenzie made the first overland link with maritime explorers.

Mackenzie paddled to Dean Channel where he used vermillion paint to leave his message on a rock in Elcho Harbour.

After achieving his ambition to find the Pacific, Mackenzie returned to Montreal in 1794. He quit the North West Company in 1799, joined the XY Company, but eventually returned to England where he was knighted in 1802. He married in 1812 and retired to a Scottish estate at Dunkeld. He died of Bright's disease on March 12, 1820.

The northern town of Mackenzie was named for Mackenzie in 1966 and a 279-mile heritage trail from Blackwater River, near Prince George, to Bella Coola was formally established in 1987 to mark Mackenzie's overland route along the "grease trail" to the Pacific. The better-known Lewis and Clark expedition, sponsored by Thomas Jefferson, reached the Pacific Ocean 12 years after Mackenzie accomplished the feat. Many Americans believe Lewis and Clark were the first "white men" to reach the Pacific by travelling overland.

Mackenzie's journey marked the end of one era of B.C. history and the commencement of another. It was only a matter of time before commerce resolved the mysteries of geography, forts were erected and European-style government was introduced.

BOOKS: The National Library of Canada has a copy of Alexander Mackenzie's *Voyages from Montreal on the River St. Lawrence through the Continent of North America, to the Frozen Pacific Oceans in the Years 1789 and 1793...* (London: Printed for T. Cadell and W. Davies [etc.] by R. Noble, 1801). It has been republished in various editions. Also: *The Letters and Journals of Sir Alexander Mackenzie*, ed. W.K. Lamb (London, 1970).

ADDITIONAL REFERENCES

Arranged chronologically by publication date

FRANCIS DRAKE:

Corbett, Julian S. *Drake and the Tudor Navy* (London, 1898).

Davidson, G. *Francis Drake on the Northwest Coast of America in the Year 1579* (San Francisco: Geographical Society of the Pacific, 1908).

Nuttall, Zelia (editor). *New Light on Drake* (London: The Hakluyt Society, 1914).

Penzer, N.M. (editor). *The World Encompassed and Analogous Contemporary Documents Concerning Sir Francis Drake's Circumnavigation of the World* (London: The Argonaut Press, 1926; New York: Cooper Square Publishers, 1969).

Wagner, Henry R. *Sir Francis Drake's Voyage Around the World: Its Aims and Achievements* (San Francisco: John Howell, 1926).

Robertson, John. *Francis Drake and Other Early Explorers Along the Pacific Coast* (San Francisco: The Grabhorn Press, 1927).

Bishop, R.P. "Drake's Course in the North Pacific" *British Columbia Historical Quarterly*, 3 (1939).

Bolton, Herbert E., et al. *The Plate of Brass: Evidence of the Visit of Francis Drake to California in the Year 1579* (San Francisco: California Historical Society, 1953).

Aker, Raymond. *Report of Findings Relating to Identification of Sir Francis Drake's Encampment at Point Reyes National Seashore* (Point Reyes, California: Drake Navigators Guild, 1970).

Wallis, Helen. *The Voyage of Sir Francis Drake Mapped in Silver and Gold* (Berkeley: Friends of the Bancroft Library, 1974).

Hart, James D. *The Plate of Brass Reexamined* (Berkeley: The Bancroft Library, University of California, 1977).

Wilson, Derek. *The World Encompassed: Francis Drake and His Great Voyage* (New York: Harper & Row, 1977).

Aker, Raymond & Edward Von der Porten. *Discovering Portus Novae Albionis: Francis Drake's California Harbor* (Palo Alto: Drake Navigators Guild, 1979).

Hanna, Warren L. *Lost Harbor: The Controversy of Drake's California Anchorage* (Berkeley and Los Angeles: University of California Press, 1979).

Hart, James D. *The Plate of Brass Reexamined, A Supplement* (Berkeley: The Bancroft Library, University of California, 1979).

Thomas, R.C. *Drake at Olomp-ali* (San Francisco: A-Pala Press, 1979).

Thrower, Norman J.W. (editor). *Francis Drake and the Famous Voyage, 1577–1580* (Berkeley: University of California Press, 1984).

Sugden, John. *Sir Francis Drake* (New York: Henry Holt and Company, 1991).

Aker, Raymond & Edward Von der Porten. *Discovering Francis Drake's California Harbor* (Palo Alto: Drake Navigators Guild, 2000).

Bawlf, R. Samuel. *Sir Francis Drake and his Secret Voyage 1577–1580* (Vancouver: Douglas & McIntyre, 2003).

RICHARD HAKLUYT:

The Principall Navigations, Voiages and Discoveries of the English Nation, Made by Sea or Ouer Land, To The Most Remote and Farthest Quarters Of The Earth at any time within the compasse of these 1500 yeeres.... (London: George Bishop and Ralph Newberie, 1589; Christopher Baker, 1659; Hakluyt Society, Peabody Museum of Salem, Cambridge University Press, 1965). Includes "The Famous Voyage of Francis Drake."

An Excellent Treatise of Antonie Galvano, Portugal, containing the most ancient and modern discoveries of the world, especially by navigation, according to the course of times from the flood until the Year of Grace, 1555. Contained within A Selection of Curious, Rare and Early Voyages, and Histories of Interesting Discoveries, published by Hakluyt (London: G. Woodfall, 1601; 1812).

A particular discourse concerning the greate necessitie and manifolde comodyities that are like to growe to this Realme of Englande by the Westerne discoveries lately attempted, written in the year 1584 (unpublished until 1877, within *The Documentary History of the State of Maine*).

RUSSIANS & NORTH AMERICA:

Müller, Gerhard Friedrich. *Nachrichten von Seereisen* (St. Petersburg, 1758). Translated by T. Jefferys as *Voyages from Asia to America, for Completing the Discoveries of the North West Coast of America* (London, 1761). Translated by Carol Furness as *Bering's Voyages: The Reports from Russia* (University of Alaska Press, 1986).

Sarychev, Gavril. *Account of a Voyage of Discovery to the North-east of Siberia, the Frozen Ocean and the North-east Sea* (1806; Amsterdam: N. Israel & New York: Da Capo Press, 1969).

Coxe, William. *Account of the Russian Discoveries between Asia and America* (London, 1780).

Bancroft, H.H. *History of Alaska* (San Francisco, 1886).

Golder, Frank A. *Russian Expansion in the Pacific, 1641–1850* (Cleveland: Arthur H. Clark, 1914; reprinted Gloucester, Massachusetts: Peter Smith, 1960).

Golder, Frank A. *Bering's Voyages*, 2 volumes (New York: American Geographical Society, 1922 and 1925; New York: Octogon Books, 1968).

Stejneger, Leonhard. *Georg Wilhelm Steller, the Pioneer of Alaskan Natural History* (Cambridge, Massachusetts: Harvard University Press, 1936).

Chevigny, Hector. *Russian America: The Great Alaskan Venture 1741–1867* (New York: Viking Press, 1965).

Michael, Henry N. *Lieutenant Zagoskin's Travels in Russian America, 1842–1844* (University of Toronto Press, 1967).

Crowhart-Vaughn, E.A.P. (editor, translator). *Explorations of Kamchatka, North Pacific Scimitar* (Portland: Western Imprints, The Press of the Oregon Historical Society, 1972).

Makarova, Raisa V. *Russians on the Pacific, 1743–1799*, edited and translated by Richard A. Pierce & Alton S. Connelly (Kingston, Ontario: Limestone Press, 1975).

Fisher, Raymond H. *Bering's Voyages: Whither and Why* (University of Washington Press, 1977).

Barratt, Glynn. *Russia in Pacific Waters, 1715–1825* (Vancouver: UBC Press, 1981).

Fisher, Raymond H. (editor). *The Voyage of Semen Dezhnev in 1648: Bering's Precursor* (London: Hakluyt Society, 1981).

Dmytryshyn, Basil & E.A.P. Crownhart-Vaughan & Thomas Vaughan (editors, translators). *Russian Penetration of the North Pacific Ocean. To Siberia and Russian America. Three Centuries of Russian Eastern Expansion 1700–1797* (Oregon Historical Society Press, 1988).

Black, J.L. & D.K. Buse (editors). *G.F Müller and Siberia 1733–1743,* transl. Victoria Joan Moessner (University of Alaska Press, 1989).

Black, Lydia. *Russians in Alaska 1732–1867* (University of Alaska Press, 2004).

SPAIN & THE PACIFIC NORTHWEST:

Chapman, Charles Edward. *The Founding of Spanish California: The Northward Expansion of New Spain, 1687–1783* (New York: Macmillan, 1916).

Mourelle, Francisco Antonio. *Journal of a Voyage in 1775,* translated by Daines Barrington (London: J. Nichols, 1781). *Voyage of the Sonora in 1775,* translated by Daines Barrington (San Francisco: Thomas Russell, 1920; Ye Galleon Press, 1995).

Wagner, H.R. *Spanish Voyages to the Northwest Coast of America in the Sixteenth Century* (San Francisco: California Historical Society, 1929; Amsterdam: N. Israel, 1968).

Wagner, H.R. *Spanish Explorations in the Strait of Juan de Fuca* (Santa Ana, California: Fine Arts Press, 1933; New York: AMS Press, 1971).

Wagner, H.R. *Cartography of the Northwest Coast of America to the Year 1800,* 2 vols. (University of California Press, 1937).

Turanzas, José Porrúa (editor). *Relación del viage hecho por las goletas Sutil y Mexicana en el año de 1792 para reconocer el Estrecho de Fuca* (Madrid: Artes Gráficos Minerva, 1958).

Bobb, Bernard E. *The Viceregency of Antonio María Buccareli in New Spain 1771–1779* (Austin: University of Texas Press, 1962).

Galvin, J. (editor). *A Journal of Explorations along the Coast from Monterey in the Year 1755* (San Francisco: John Howell Books, 1964).

Cutter, Donald C. & Laurio H. Destéfani. *Tadeo Haenke y el final de una vieja polémica* (Buenos Aires, 1966).

Thurman, Michael E. *The Naval Department of San Blas, New Spain's Bastion for Alta California and Nootka, 1767–1798* (Glendale, California: Arthur H. Clark Co., 1967).

Mathes, W. Michael. *Vizcaino and Spanish Expansion in the Pacific Ocean 1580–1630* (San Francisco: California Historical Society, 1968).

Cutter, Donald C. (editor). *The California Coast: A Bilingual Edition of Documents from the Sutro Collection,* translated and edited in 1891 by George Butler Griffin (University of Oklahoma Press, 1969).

Cook, Warren L. *Flood Tide of Empire: Spain and the Pacific Northwest, 1543–1819* (New Haven: Yale University Press, 1973).

Colecciones de Diarios y Relaciones para la Historia de los Viajes y Descubrimientos, VII: Comprende los viajes de Arteaga en 1792 y de Caamaño en 1792, por la costa NO. de America, Consejo Superior de Investigaciones Ceintíficas (Instituto Historico de Marina, 1975).

Fireman, Janet R. *The Spanish Royal Corps of Engineers in the Western Borderlands, 1764 to 1815* (Glendale, California: Arthur H. Clark Co., 1977).

Engstrand, Iris H. H. *Spanish Scientists in the New World: The Eighteenth-Century Expeditions* (Seattle: University of Washington Press, 1981).

Kendrick, John S. *The Men With Wooden Feet: The Spanish Exploration of the Pacific Northwest* (Toronto: NC Press, 1986).

Cutter, Donald C. *Malaspina and Galiano: Spanish Voyages to the Northwest Coast, 1791 & 1792* (University of Washington Press/Douglas & McIntyre, 1991).

Bartroli, Tomas. *Brief Presence: Spain's Activity on America's Northwest Coast, 1774–1796* (Vancouver: Self-published, 1991).

Kendrick, John S. (editor). *The Voyage of the Sutil and Mexicana, 1792* (Spokane: Arthur H. Clark Co., 1991).

Bartroli, Tomas. *Genesis of Vancouver City, Explorations of its Site–1791, 1792 & 1808* (Vancouver: Self-published, 1992; 1997).

Inglis, Robin (editor). *Spain and the North Pacific Coast* (Vancouver Maritime Museum, 1992).

ALEJANDRO MALASPINA:

Espinosa y Tello, José. *Memorias sobre las observaciones astronómicas hechas por los navegantes españoles en distintos lugares del globo* (1809).

Novo y Colson, Pedro. *Viaje político científico alrededor del mundo por las corbetas Descubierta y Atrevida, al mando de los capitanes de navío Don Alejandro Malaspina y Don José Bustamante* (1885).

Caselli, Carlo. *Alessandro Malaspina e la sua spedizione scientifica intorno al mondo* (Milano, 1929).

Fernández, Justino (editor). *Tomás de Suría y su Viaje con Malaspina, 1791* (Mexico City: Librería de Porrúa Hermanos y Cía, 1939).

Morse, William Inglis. *Letters of Alejandro Malaspina* (Boston: McIver-Johnson Co., 1944).

Cutter, Donald C. *Malaspina in California* (San Francisco: John Howell, 1960).

Palau Baquero, Mercedes. *Catálogo de los dibujos, aguandas y acuarelas de la expedición Malaspina* (Madrid: Museo de América, 1980).

Sotos Serrano, Carmen. *Los Pintores de la Expedición de Alejandro Malaspina*, 2 vols. (Madrid: Real Academia de la Histiria,1982).

Manfredi, Dario. *Alessandro Malaspina…Le inclinazioni scientfiche e reiformatrici* (La Spezia: Centro Alessandro Malaspina, 1984).

Palau Baquero, Mercedes & Aránzazu Zabala & Blanca Sáiz (editors). *Viaje científico y político a la America Meridional…en los años de 1789, 90, 91, 92, y 95…por los capitanes de navío D. Alejandro Malaspina y D. José Bustamante* (Madrid: Museo Universal, 1984).

Painted in 1938, E.J. Hughes' fanciful depiction of "Captain Malaspina sketching the sandstone 'Galleries' on Gabriola Island" was one of several historical murals in the dining room of Nanaimo's Malaspina Hotel prior to its demolition in the 1990s.

Capellini, Giovanni (editor). *Alessandro Malaspina: Studi e documenti per le biografia del navigante* (La Spezia: Centro Alessandro Malaspina, 1985).

Manfredi, Dario. *Sugli anni "Prontremolesi" di Alessandro Malaspina* (La Spezia: Centro Alessandro Malaspina, 1986).

Higueras Rodríguez, Dolores. *Catálogo crítico de los documentos de la expedición Malaspina*, 2 vols. (Madrid: Museo Naval, 1987).

Manfredi, Dario. *L'inchiesta dell'inquisitore sule eresie di Alessandro Malaspina* (La Spezia: Centro Alessandro Malaspina, 1987).

Poupeney de Hart, Catherine. *Relations de l'expédition Malaspina, Préambule* (Montreal: Longueuil, 1987).

Cerezo Martínez, Ricardo. *La Expedición Malaspina, 1789–1794* (Madrid: Ministerio de Defensa, Museo Naval, Lunwerg Editores, 1988).

González Claverán, Virginia. *Expedición científica de Malaspina en Nueva España* (Colegio de México, 1988).

Manfredi, Dario. *Sugli studi e sulle navigazioni "Minori" di Alessandro Malaspina* (La Spezia: Centro Alessandro Malaspina, 1988).

Cerezo Martínez, Ricardo (editor). *Diario General del Viaje, La Expedición Malaspina*, 2 vols. (Madrid: Ministerio de Defensa, Museo Naval, Lunwerg Editores, 1990).

Manfredi, Dario. *Sugli introduttivo del tradadito sobre el valor* (La Spezia: Centro Alessandro Malaspina, 1990).

Higueras Rodríguez, Dolores. *Iconographic Album of the Malaspina Expedition* (Madrid: Museo Naval, 1991).

Higueras Rodríguez, Dolores & Maria Luisa Martín-Merás. *Relación del viaje hecho por las Goletas Sutil y Mexicana en el año 1792 para reconocer el Estrecho de Juan de Fuca*, 2 vols. (Madrid: 1802; Madrid: Museo Naval, 1991).

Beerman, Eric. *El diario del proceso y encarcelamiento de Alejandro Malaspina* (Madrid: Editorial Naval, 1992).

Sáiz Martínez, Blanca. *Bibliografía sobre Alejandro Malaspina* (Museo Universal, 1992).

Sáiz Martínez, Blanca (editor). *Alejandro Malaspina: La América imposible* (Madrid: Compañía Literaria, 1994).

Kendrick, John S. *Alejandro Malaspina: Portrait of a Visionary* (McGill-Queen's University Press, 1999).

LA PÉROUSE:

Allen, Edward Webber. *The Vanishing Frenchman: The Mysterious Disappearance of Lapérouse* (Rutland, Vermont: C.D. Tuttle, Co., 1959).

Rudkin, Charles N. *The First French Expedition to California: La Pérouse in 1786* (Los Angeles: Glen Dawson, 1959).

Dunmore, John. *Pacific Explorer, The Life of Jean François de la Pérouse 1741–1788* (Annapolis, Maryland: Naval Institute Press, 1985).

Inglis, Robin. *The Lost Voyage of Lapérouse* (Vancouver Maritime Museum, 1986).

Dunmore, John (editor, translator). *The Journal of Jean-François de Galaup de la Pérouse, 1785–1788*, volume I (Hakluyt Society, 1994), volume II (Hakluyt Society, 1995).

JAMES COOK:

A Voyage to the Pacific Ocean. Undertaken, by the Command of his Majesty, for making Discoveries in the Northern Hemisphere. To determine The Position and Extent of the West Side of North America; its Distance from Asia; and the Practicability of a Northern Passage to Europe. Performed under the direction of Captains Cook, Clerke, and Gore, In His Majesty's Ships the Resolution and Discovery. In the Years 1776, 1777, 1778, 1779, and 1780. In Three Volumes. Vol. I and II written by James Cook, F.R.S. Vol. III by Captain James King, LL.D. and F.R.S. Edited by Dr. John Douglas, Canon of Windsor and St. Paul's. First Edition. Three quarto volumes and one folio atlas, with 87 engravings. (London: Printed by W. and A. Strahan for G. Nicol, and T. Cadell, 1784). The National Library of Canada retains a copy of this book.

Beaglehole, J.C. (editor). *The Journals of Captain Cook, Vol. I, Endeavour* (Cambridge University Press for the Hakluyt Society, 1955). *The Journals of Captain Cook, Vol. II, Resolution, Adventure* (Cambridge University Press for the Hakluyt Society, 1961). *The Journals of Captain James Cook, Vol. III, The Voyage of the Resolution and Discovery 1776–1780* (Cambridge University Press for the Hakluyt Society, 1967). *The Journals of Captain Cook. Vol. III. Parts 1 & 2, Resolution and Discovery* contains Anderson's journal and extracts from the journals of Clerke, Burney, Williamson, Edgar and King.

Edwards, Philip (editor). *The Journals of Captain Cook* (Penguin, 1999).

The first European resident, John MacKay, wintered at Tahsis with Chief Maquinna in 1786.

ALSO:

Kippis, Andrew. *The Life of Captain James Cook* (London, 1788). Republished as *A Narrative of the Voyages Round the World performed by Captain James Cook with an account of his life during the previous and intervening periods* (London, 1842).

Low, Charles R. *Captain Cook's Three Voyages Round the World* (London, 1876).

Kitson, Arthur. *Captain James Cook R.N., F.R.S. The Circumnavigtor* (London: John Murray, 1907).

Carruthers, Sir Joseph. *Captain James Cook, R.N., One Hundred and Fifty Years After* (New York: E.P. Dutton and Co., 1930).

Howay, F.W. (editor). *Zimmerman's Captain Cook, 1781* (Toronto: Ryerson, 1930).

Stokes, J.F.G. *Origin of the Condemnation of Captain Cook in Hawaii* (London, 1930).

Gould, Rupert T. *Captain Cook* (London, 1935).

Campbell, Gordon, Vice-Admiral. *Captain James Cook, R.N., F.R.S.* (London, 1936).

Carrington, Hugh. *The Life of Captain Cook* (1939; London: Sedgewick & Jackson, 1967).

Muir, John Reid. *The Life & Achievements of Captain James Cook, R.N., F.R.S., Explorer, Navigator, Surveyor & Physician* (London: Blackie & Son, 1939).

Lloyd, Christopher (editor). *The Voyages of Captain Cook Selected from his Journals* (London: The Cresset Press, 1949).

Homes, Sir M. *Captain Cook R.N., F.R. S.: A Bibliographical Excursion* (London, 1952).

Price, A. Grenfell (editor). *The Explorations of Captain James Cook in the Pacific* (1958; Sydney, Australia: Angus & Robertson, 1969).

Villiers, Alan. *Captain Cook* (London: Hodder and Stoughton, 1967).

Beaglehorne, John Cawte. *Captain Cook and Captain Bligh* (University of Wellington, N.Z., 1967).

Rienits, Rex & Thea. *The Voyages of Captain Cook* (London, New York: Paul Hamlyn, 1968).

Dale, Paul W. *Seventy North to Fifty South–Captain Cook's Last Voyage* (New Jersey: Prentice Hall, 1969).

Bushnell, O.A. *The Return of Lono: A Novel of Captain Cook's Last Voyage* (Honolulu, 1971).

Syme, Ronald & Warner Forman. *The Travels of Captain Cook* (New York, London: McGraw-Hill, 1971).

MacLean, Alistair. *Captain Cook* (William Collins Sons, 1972).

Beaglehole, J.C. *The Life of Captain Cook* (London: Adam & Charles Black, 1974).

Conner, D. & L. Miller. *Master Mariner: Captain James Cook & the Peoples of the Pacific* (Douglas & McIntyre, 1978).

Greenhill, Basil. *James Cook: The Opening of the Pacific* (Palo Alto: Pendragon House, 1978).

Efrat, Barbara & J. Langlois (editors). *Captain Cook and The Spanish Explorers in the Coast* Volume VII, No. I (Sound Heritage, Royal B.C. Museum, 1978).

Innes, Hammond. *The Last Voyage: Captain Cook's Lost Diary* (London: Collins, 1978).

Kennedy, Gavin. *The Death of Captain Cook* (London: Gerald Duckworth & Co. Ltd., 1978).

Fisher, Robin & Hugh Johnston (editors). *Captain James Cook and His Times* (University of Washington Press, 1979).

Gray, William R. *Voyages to Paradise: Exploring in the Wake of Captain Cook* (Washington D.C.: National Geographic Society, 1981).

Joppien, Rudiger & Bernard Smith. *The Art of Captain Cook's Voyages, The Voyage of the Resolution and Discovery 1776–1780* (Yale University Press, 1988).

David, Andrew. *The Charts and Coastal Views of Captain Cook's Voyages: Vol. 1, The Voyage of the Endeavour, 1768–1771* (Hakluyt Society, 1988).

Cordingly, D. *Captain Cook Navigator* (London: National Maritime Museum, 1988).

Withey, Lynne. *Voyages of Discovery: Captain Cook and the Exploration of the Pacific* (University of California Press, 1989).

David, Andrew. *The Charts and Coastal Views of Captain Cook's Voyages: Vol. 2, The Voyage of Resolution and Adventure, 1771–1775* (Hakluyt Society, 1992).

Hough, Richard. *Captain James Cook* (Coronet, 1995).

David, Andrew. *Charts and Coastal Views of Captain Cook's Voyages: Vol. 3, The Voyage of the Resolution and Discovery, 1776–1780* (Hakluyt Society, 1997).

Barrow, John (editor). *The Voyages of Captain Cook* (Wordsworth Editions Ltd, 1999).

Villiers, Alan. *Captain Cook: The Seamen's Seaman* (Penguin Books, 2001).

Collingridge, Vanessa. *Captain Cook: Obsession and Betrayal in the New World* (Ebury Press, 2002).

King, John Bolton. *James King R.N.* (Exeter: South West Maritime History Soc., 2004).

JOHN LEDYARD:

Sparks, Jared. *Life of John Ledyard, the American Traveller; Comprising Selections from His Journals and Correspondence* (London: Hilliard and Brown, 1828, 1834, 1847, 1864).

Mumford, J. K. *John Ledyard: An American Marco Polo* (Portland: Binfords & Mort, 1939).

Mumford, J. K. (editor). *John Ledyard's Journal of Captain Cook's Last Voyage* (Corvalis, Oregon: Oregon State University, 1963).

Watrous, Stephen D. (editor). *John Ledyard's Journey Through Russia and Siberia 1787–1788: The Journal and Selected Letters* (Madison: University of Wisconsin Press, 1966).

NOOTKA SOUND (ARTICLES):

Howay, F. W. "The Spanish Settlement at Nootka," *The Washington Historical Quarterly* VIII (1917): 163–171.

Kuykendall, Ralph S. "James Colnett and the Princess Royal," *The Quarterly of the Oregon Historical Society* XXV (1924): 36–52.

Howay, F. W. "Some Additional Notes Upon Captain Colnett and the *Princess Royal*," *The Quarterly of the Oregon Historical Society* XXVI (1925): 12–22.

Brunhouse, R. L. (editor). "An American at Nootka Sound, 1789," *Pacific Northwest Quarterly* XXXI (1940): 285–286.

Moeller, Beverley B. "Captain James Colnett and the Tsimshian Indians, 1787," *Pacific Northwest Quarterly* 57 (1966): 13–17.

Kaplanoff, Mark D. (editor). "Nootka Sound in 1789: Joseph Ingraham's Account," *Pacific Northwest Quarterly* 65 (1974): 157–163.

Archer, Christon I. "Retreat from the North: Spain's Withdrawal from Nootka Sound, 1793–1795," *BC Studies* 37 (1978): 19-36.

214

Efrat, Barbara S. & W.J. Langlois (editors). "Nu-tka: Captain Cook and the Spanish Explorers on the Coast," *Sound Heritage* VII, No. 1 (1978).

Efrat, Barbara S. & W.J. Langlois (editors). "Nu-tka: The History and Survival of Nootkan Culture," *Sound Heritage* VII, No. 2 (1978).

Mathes, Valerie Sherer. "Wickaninnish, a Clayoquot Chief, as Recorded by Early Travelers," *Pacific Northwest Quarterly* 70 (1979): 110–120.

McMillan, Alan D. "Archaeological Research in Nootka Territory: Barkley Sound to the Alberni Valley," *BC Studies* 48 (1980/81): 86–102.

Fireman, Janet R. "The Seduction of George Vancouver: A Nootka Affair," *Pacific Historical Review* LVI (1987): 427–443.

JOHN MEARES:
Morgan, Murray C. *The John Meares Expeditions: The Last Wilderness* (University of Washington Press, 1955).

Howay, F.W. *The Dixon-Meares Controversy* (Amsterdam: N. Israel, 1969).

Nokes, J. Richard & David L. Nicandri. *Almost a Hero: The Voyages of John Meares, R.N., to China, Hawaii and the Northwest Coast* (Pullman, Washington: WSU Press, 1998).

GEORGE VANCOUVER:
Meany, Edmond S. (editor). *A New Vancouver Journal on the Discovery of Puget Sound, By [Edward Bell] a Member of Chatham's Crew* (Seattle: University of Washington, 1915).

Anderson, George Howard. *Vancouver and his Great Voyage; The Story of a Norfolk Sailor, Captain Geo. Vancouver, R.N., 1757–1798* (King's Lynn, Thew & Son, 1923).

Godwin, George. *Vancouver: A Life 1757–1798* (London: Philip Allan, 1930).

Marshall, J. Stirrat & C. Marshall. *Adventure in Two Hemispheres including Captain Vancouver's Voyage* (Vancouver: Talex Printing, 1955). Republished as *Vancouver's Voyage* (Mitchell Press, 1967).

Meany, E. S. *Vancouver's Discovery of Puget Sound* (Portland: Binfords & Mort, 1957).

Anderson, Bern. *Surveyor of the Sea: The Life and Voyages of Captain George Vancouver* (University of Washington, 1960).

Fisher, Robin. *Vancouver's Voyage: Charting the Northwest Coast, 1791–1795* (Douglas & McIntrye, 1992).

Gillespie, Brenda Guild. *On Stormy Seas: The Triumphs and Torments of George Vancouver* (Horsdal & Schubart, 1992).

Fisher, Robin & Hugh Johnston. *From Maps to Metaphors: The Pacific World of George Vancouver* (UBC Press, 1993).

ALEXANDER MACKENZIE:

Hardwick, Francis C. (editor). *The Helping Hand: How Indian Canadians Helped Alexander Mackenzie Reach the Pacific Ocean* (Center for Continuing Education: Indian Education Resources Center, University of British Columbia, 1972).

Hardwick, Francis Chester & Phillip Moir & Sister Mary Paul. *The Helping Hand: The Debt of Alexander Mackenzie and Simon Fraser to Indian Canadians* (Tantalus Research, 1973).

Mead, Robert Douglas. *Ultimate North: Canoeing Mackenzie's Great River* (Garden City, New York: Doubleday, 1976).

Smith, James K. *Alexander Mackenzie* (Fitzhenry & Whiteside, 1976).

Fawcett, Brian. *The Secret Journal of Alexander Mackenzie* (Talonbooks, 1985).

Woodworth, John & Hälle Flygare. *In the Steps of Alexander Mackenzie: Trail Guide*, 2nd ed., enlarged and updated (Kelowna: Self-published, 1987).

Manson, Ainslie. *Alexander Mackenzie* (Grolier, 1988).

Hing, Robert J., *Tracking Mackenzie to the Sea: Coast to Coast in Eighteen Splashdowns* (Manassas, Virginia: Anchor Watch Press, 1992).

Xydes, Georgia. *Alexander Mackenzie and the Explorers of Canada* (New York: Chelsea House, 1992).

Manson, Ainslie. *A Dog Came, Too: A True Story* (Toronto: Groundwood, 1993).

Gough, Barry M. *First Across the Continent: Sir Alexander Mackenzie* (McClelland & Stewart, 1997).

GENERAL:

Bancroft, Hubert Howe [& Henry L. Oak & Frances Fuller Victor]. *History of the Northwest Coast*, 2 vols. (San Francisco: A.L. Bancroft and Co., 1884).

Dahlgren, E.W. *The Discovery of the Hawaiian Islands* (Stockholm: Almquist & Wiksells, 1916; New York: AMS Press, 1977).

Caughey, John Walton. *History of the Pacific Coast* (Los Angeles: Self-published, 1933).

Beaglehole. J.C. *The Exploration of the Pacific* (London: Adam and Charles Black, 1934; Stanford: Stanford University Press, 1968).

Howay, F.W. *Voyages of the Columbia* (Harvard, 1941; New York: Da Capo Press, 1969).

Keithahn, Edward. *Monuments in Cedar: The Authentic Story of the Totem Pole* (Ketchikan, Alaska: Roy Anderson, 1945; Seattle: Superior Publishing Company, 1963).

Drucker, Philip. *The Northern and Central Nootkan Tribes* (U.S. Government Printing Office, 1951). Based on field research conducted 1935–36.

Drucker, Philip. *Indians of the Northwest Coast* (American Museum of Natural History and McGraw-Hill, 1955).

Krause, Aurel. *The Tlingit Indians*, translated by Erna Gunther (University of Washington Press, 1956).

Barbeau, Marius. *Pathfinders in the North Pacific* (Toronto: Ryerson, 1958).

Barabash-Nikiforov, I. I. *The Sea Otter* (London: Oldbourne Press, 1962).

Duff, Wilson. *The Impact of the White Man* (Victoria: Provincial Museum, 1964). Republished as *The Indian History of British Columbia: The Impact of the White Man* (Victoria: Royal British Columbia Museum, 1992, 1997).

Gunther, Erna. *Indian Life on the Northwest Coast of North America as seen by the Early Explorers and Fur Traders during the Last Decades of the Eighteenth Century* (University of Chicago Press, 1972).

Akrigg, G.P.V. & Helen B. Akrigg. *British Columbia Chronicle 1778–1846* (Vancouver: Discovery Press, 1975).

Pethick, Derek. *First Approaches to the Northwest Coast* (Douglas & McIntyre, 1976).

Senders, John. *The Nootkan Indian: A Pictorial* (Alberni Valley Museum, 1977).

Woodcock, George. *Peoples of the Coast: The Indians of the Pacific Northwest* (Hurtig, 1977).

Pethick, Derek. *The Nootka Connection* (Douglas & McIntyre, 1980).

Vaughan, Thomas & Bill Holm. *Soft Gold: The Fur Trade and Cultural Exchange on the Northwest Coast of America* (Portland: Oregon Historical Society, 1982, 1990).

Derek Pethick

Charles Lillard

Derek Hayes

Glyndwr Williams

Henry, John Frazier. *Early Maritime Artists of the Pacific Northwest Coast, 1741–1841* (University of Washington Press, 1984).

Cole, Douglas. *Captured Heritage: The Scramble for Northwest Coast Artifacts* (Douglas & McIntyre, 1985).

Lillard, Charles. *The Ghostland People: A Documentary History of the Queen Charlotte Islands, 1859–1906* (Victoria: Sono Nis, 1989).

Little, C.H. *18th Century Maritime Influences on the History and Place Names of British Columbia* (Madrid: Editorial Naval, 1991).

Gibson, James. *Otter Skins, Boston Ships, and China Goods: The Maritime Fur Trade of the Northwest Coast, 1785–1841* (McGill-Queen's, 1992).

Gough, Barry. *The Northwest Coast: British Navigation Trade and Discoveries to 1812* (UBC Press, 1992).

Johnston, Hugh (editor). *The Pacific Province: A History of British Columbia* (Douglas & McIntyre, 1996).

McDowell, Jim. *Hamatsa: The Enigma of Cannibalism on the Pacific Northwest Coast* (Ronsdale, 1997).

Malloy, Mary. *A Most Remarkable Enterprise: Maritime Commerce & Culture on the Northwest Coast* (Parnassus Imprints, 1997).

Malloy, Mary. *Souvenirs of the Fur Trade: Northwest Coast Indian Art and Artifacts, 1788–1844* (University of Alaska Press, 1998).

Hayes, Derek. *Historical Atlas of British Columbia and the Pacific Northwest* (Cavendish Books, 1999).

Brown, Steven C. (editor). *Spirits of the Water: Native Art Collected on Expeditions to Alaska and British Columbia, 1774–1910* (University of Washington Press, 2000).

Glavin, Terry. *The Last Great Sea: A Voyage through the Human and Natural History of the North Pacific Ocean* (Vancouver: Suzuki Foundation, Greystone Books, 2000).

Brown, Steven & Lloyd J. Averill. *Sun Dogs & Eagle Down: The Indian Paintings of Bill Holm* (University of Washington Press, Douglas & McIntyre, 2000).

Hayes, Derek. *Historical Atlas of the North Pacific Ocean* (North Pacific Marine Science Organization, Douglas & McIntyre, 2001).

Bolanz, Maria & Gloria C. Williams. *Tlingit Art: Totem Poles & Art of the Alaskan Indians* (Surrey: Hancock House, 2003).

Koppel, Tom. *Lost World: Rewriting Prehistory–How New Science is Tracing America's Ice Age Mariners* (Atria Books, 2003).

Keddie, Grant. *Songhees Pictorial: A History of the Songhees People as Seen by Outsiders, 1790–1912* (Victoria: Royal BC Museum, 2003).

Williams, Glyndwr. *Voyages of Delusion: The Search for the Northwest Passage* (Yale University Press, 2003).

ADDENDA

1736 –

The first book to describe any part of Alaska was by French geographer Jean-Baptiste du Halde in his 4-volume general history of China, *Description Geographique, Historique, Chronologique, Politique et Physique de de l'Empire de la China et de la Tartarie Chinoise* (Paris: 1735). Translated and reprinted in The Hague and London in 1736, it contained a copy of the first report submitted by Vitus Bering when he reached St. Petersburg in 1730. Bering had reached St. Lawrence Island, now part of Alaska, but he never reached the American mainland.

1751 –

German scientist Johann Georg Gmelin (1709–1755) published a 4-volume work about Siberia, *Reise durch Sibirien, von dem jahr 1733 bis 1743* (Göttingen, 1751-1752), in which he provided details of Bering's voyages. In 1733, Gmelin set out with Gerhard Müller on an overland expedition under the general command of Vitus Bering to obtain scientific information. Although he never reached Kamchatka, Gmelin was absent from the Academy of Sciences in St. Petersburg for ten years. Upon his return to Germany, Gmelin completed his extensive work, ignoring the demand for secrecy from his former Russian employers because he was writing in Germany.

1753 –

Gerhard Müller is suspected of being the author of the second significant report of Bering's fatal voyage, a 60-page pamphlet entitled *A Letter from a Russian Sea-Officer*. First published in French in Berlin in 1753 as *Lettre d'un Officier de la Marine Russienne*, it was translated as *A Letter from a Russian Sea-Officer...Containing His Remarks Upon Mr. de l'Isle's Chart and Memoir, Relative to the New Discoveries Northward and Eastward from Kamchatka* (London, 1754). This English version included a letter from Arthur Dobbs regarding the French geographer mentioned in the title.

1775 –

In addition to Bruno de Hezeta's diary account of the first European expedition known to have set foot in the Pacific Northwest—prior to Captain Cook at Nootka Sound in 1778—two accounts by priests were retrieved from archives in the 20th century. These are A.J. Baker's translation of Benito de la Sierra's journal as *The Hezeta Expedition to the Northwest Coast in 1775* (San Francisco: California Historical Quarterly, 1930), introduced by H.R. Wagner, and Miguel de la Campos' *A Journal of Explorations Northward Along the Coast from Monterey in the Year 1775* (San Francisco: John Howell, 1964), edited by John Galvin.

1780 –

British antiquarian and linguist William Coxe (1747–1828), eldest son of the king's household physician, was a Senior Fellow of King's College at Cambridge and later Archdeacon of Wiltshire. He visited St. Petersburg and later published four editions of an important summary of Russian maritime explorations. Much of his work was originally based on a German compilation published in Hamburg by Johann L. Schulze in 1776. The first

Coxe edition was *Account of the Russian Discoveries Between Asia and America. To which are added the Conquest of Siberia and the History of the Transactions and Commerce Between Russia and China* (London: 1780; 3rd edition 1787; 4th edition 1803). The third edition added "A Comparative View of the Russian Discoveries with Those Made by Captains Cook and Clerke." Coxe's later work encouraged more British investment in the exploration of the North Pacific because it confirmed the observations of James Cook in Cook's journals regarding the extent and potential value of the North Pacific fur trade. Two French translations appeared in 1781 and a German one in 1783. Coxe provided accounts of the voyages of Shalaurof, 1761–1763; Sind, 1764–1768; and Krenitzin and Levashef, 1764–1771; and others.

1785 to 1794 –
Born in Turnham Green, near London, around 1758, Joseph Billings served on the *Discovery* under Cook during his final voyage that visited Nootka Sound in 1778. Billings afterwards joined the Russian navy and was placed in charge of two Russian ships sent secretly to explore and map Siberia and Alaska. At Kamchatka, Billings visited the grave of Captain Clerke, the commander who first took over from Cook after Cook was killed in Hawaii. As the secretary for Billing's Russian expedition, Martin Sauer wrote *An Account of a Geographical and Astronomical Expedition to the Northern Parts of Russia...and of the Islands to the Eastern Ocean, Stretching to the American Coast...1785–94, performed by Commodore Joseph Billings* (London: A. Strahan, 1802; Amsterdam: N. Israel, 1968). It recorded the presence of Spaniards who were trading with both Indians and Russians, sometimes serving as middlemen between the two factions.

1789 to 1794 –
One of the most obscure documents pertaining to pre-1800 exploration of B.C. is an unoffocial account by Francisco J. de Viana, subaltern of Alejandro Malaspina, available in Spanish as *Diario del Viage Explorador de las Corbetas...Descubierta y Atrevida...1789–1794* (Madrid, 1849).

1790 –
In 1785, John Cadman Etches, Nathaniel Portlock, George Dixon, and five others formed the King George's Sound Company, otherwise known as Richard Cadman Etches & Company because John's brother, Richard Cadman Etches, was the main investor. The company obtained a five-year trading license from the South Sea Company. John Cadman Etches served as supercargo on James Colnett's *Prince of Wales* from 1786 to 1788. He and his brother Richard met with John Meares in Macao and formed a new partnership in January of 1789 called the Associated Merchants of London and India Trading to the Northwest Coast of America. John Etches was apprehended at Nootka Sound by Martínez in May of 1789 when English ships were confiscated. He published his side of the story in *An Authentic Statement of All the Facts Relative to Nootka Sound* (London: Debret, 1790).

1791 –
John Henry Cox left London in the 152-ton *Mercury* and scoured the Pacific for trading opportunities, visiting the Alaska coastline and islands in 1789. He is presumed to have changed the *Mercury*'s name to *Gustavus* and sailed under Swedish colours. According to F.W. Howay, its presence on the coast in 1790, as *Gustavus III*, is doubtful as it rests on the uncorroborated statement of John Meares on July 3, 1790. Cox's lieutenant on the *Mercury*, George Mortimer, published *Observations and remarks made during a voyage to the Islands of Teneriffe, Amsterdam, Maria's Island near Van Diemen's Land, Otaheite, Sandwich Islands, Owhyhee, the Fox Islands on the north west coast of America, Tinian, and from thence to Canton in the brig Mercury commanded by John Henry Cox* (Dublin, London, 1791; Amsterdam: Bibl. Australiana, 1975; Ye Galleon Press, 1995).

РОССІЙСКАГО КУПЦА.

ГРИГОРЬЯ

ШЕЛЕХОВА

СТРАНСТВОВАНІЕ

въ 1783 году

Изъ Охотска по Восточному Окея-
ну къ Американскимъ берегамъ,

*Съ обстоятельнымъ увѣдомленіемъ объ
открытіи новообрѣтенныхъ имъ острововъ
Кыктака и Афагнака, и съ пріобщеніемъ
описанія образа жизни, нравовъ, обрядовъ,
жилищъ и одеждъ тамошнихъ народовъ, поко-
рившихся подъ Россійскую державу: также
Климатъ, годовыя перемѣны, звѣри, домаш-
нія животныя, рыбы, птицы, земныя про-
израстѣнія и многіе другіе любопытные
предметы тамъ находящіеся, что все вѣр-
но и точно описано имъ самимъ.*

Съ чертежемъ и со изображеніемъ самаго
мореходца, и найденныхъ имъ дикихъ людей.

ВЪ САНКТПЕТЕРБУРГѢ 1791 года.
Иждивеніемъ В. С.

Russian edition of Shelekhov's account of his voyages, published in 1791.

1791 –

Having established the first permanent settlement in the Pacific Northwest at Kodiak in Alaska in 1784, Grigor Shelekhov (or Shelikov) published a slim octavo of 76 pages with a very long title, anglicized as *The Voyage of Gregory Shelekhov, a Russian Merchant, in the Year 1783, from Okhotsk over the Eastern Ocean to the American Shores; with a Circumstantial Account of the Discovery of the Islands of Kyktak and Afagnak Newly Found by Him; to which is added a Description of the Way of Life, the Customs, the Observances, the Habitations and the Dress of the Peoples Who Have Submitted Themselves to the Russian Dominion; also of the Climate, of the Yearly Changes, of the Beasts, Domestic Animals, Fishes, Birds, Plants and of Many Other Curious Objects Found Therein, All of which is Faithfully and Accurately Described by Himself. With a Map and a Representation of the Traveller Himself, and of the Savages Found by Him* (St. Petersburg, 1791). It was partially translated in London in 1795.

1791 –

As a pilot for a Spanish expedition that charted the Juan de Fuca and Georgia Straits, José Maria Narváez commanded a small schooner, the *Santa Saturnina*, that reached Spanish Banks in Vancouver in July of 1791, before any other European mariner. Journals by his two commanding officers Francisco de Eliza and Manuel Quimper were translated and edited by Henry R. Wagner within *Spanish Explorations in the Strait of Juan de Fuca* (Santa Ana, California, 1933). Narváez was born in Cadiz in 1768 and died in Guadalajara in 1840. His activities in the Pacific Northwest were extensive but there is not a published journal by Narváez or a biography to immortalize his achievements.

1792 –

Sailing with the expedition led by Dionisio Alcalá Galiano and Cayetano Valdés Flores Bazán y Péon (1762–1835) that reached Nootka Sound in 1792 in the *Sutil* and *Mexicana*, José de Espinosa y Tello participated in the last major Spanish voyage to the Pacific Northwest in the 18th century. An astronomer after whom Espinosa Inlet and Little Espinosa are named, he has been incorrectly identified as the author of *Relacion de Viage Hecho por las Goletas Sutil y Mexicana en al Ano de 1792, para Reconocer el Estecho de Fuca...* (Madrid, 1802). This work contains an exceptional historical summary of the preceding Spanish visits contributed by, but not credited to, M.F. de Navarette.

1793 –

The first artist to provide individual portraits of the Haida was Sigismund Bacstrom who sailed aboard the *Three Brothers* under Captain William Adler in 1793. There is no surviving journal for the voyage but Bacstrom's eight portraits are inscribed with the names of his subjects, plus information on where they were drawn and when. He was the first European to record the names of Haida women. Some of the other artists who visited the Pacific Northwest prior to 1800, as mentioned in the foreword, sailed with the following naval commanders: Pierre Blondela (La Pérouse), Gaspard Duché de Vancy (La Pérouse), Zachary Mudge (Vancouver), Thomas Heddington (Vancouver), Harry Humphreys (Vancouver) and John Sykes (Vancouver).

Sketch by Zachary Mudge, engraving by B.T. Pouncy: "Discovery on the Rocks in Queen Charlotte's Sound."

1799 –

After 25 years of commerce between Euro-Americans and Haida, by the late 1790s it had become established practice for Haida villages and fur-trading expeditions to exchange hostages as a peace bond between their cultures. Samuel Burling sailed from Boston in 1798. As a clerk for Captain James Rowan on the *Eliza*, he twice served as a willing hostage in villages on the Queen Charlotte Islands. He produced some drawings of the Haida villages and his fair-minded but seldom-cited 1799 journal of his adventures and observations was later made available by the Massachusetts Historical Society. There are few details known about Burling's origins.

1799 –

Richard J. Cleveland arrived in the Pacific Northwest with a "dubious crew" from the South China coast for a four-year fur-trading expedition on the brig *Caroline*. As a twenty-five-year-old entrepreneur from Salem, Massachusetts, Cleveland described Tlingits he saw in the waters around the north end of the Queen Charlotte Islands and Sitka, Alaska in March of 1799 as a "more hideous set of beings, in the form of men and women I had never before seen," with some groups looking "as if they had escaped from the dominions of Satan himself." Cleveland's xenophobia prevented him from wondering why some of the Indians might appear "restless" or hostile when, in fact, another ship had recently visited the same waters and, fearing attack, had fired upon the Tlingit without provocation. In 1803 Cleveland went into partnership with Captain Shaler on the *Lelia Byrd*. His rare memoir from the perspective of an American crewman is *A Narrative of Voyages and Commercial Enterprises*, 2 vols. (Cambridge, Massachusetts: John Owen, 1842, 1843). Born in 1773, Cleveland died in 1860.

1799 –

One of the earliest attempts to create a phonetic dictionary of coastal language in British Columbia was made by a young American sailor named William F. Sturgis who visited the West Coast in 1799, at age seventeen. Sturgis was born on February 25, 1782 in Barnstable, Massachusetts where his father William E. Sturgis was a ship master. Upon the death of his father in 1797, he was forced to go to sea to support the family. His employers at J. & T.H. Perkins were despatching the *Eliza* to the North Pacific and China. Sturgis acted as assistant trader and was so good in this position that he was selected as chief mate of the *Ulysses*. He then sailed under Captain Charles Derby in the *Caroline*. When Derby died, Sturgis took command. He returned to Boston in 1810 and with John Bryant formed the house of Bryant & Sturgis. From 1810 to 1850, much of the trade carried on with the Pacific Northwest coast and China was under Sturgis' direction. Sturgis was also known for his proficiency in Latin. He took great interest in public affairs, especially relating to the Pacific Northwest. For almost 30 years he was a member of the Massachusetts House or Senate. He was President of the Boston Marine Society and a member of the Massachusetts Historical Society. The firm of Bryant & Sturgis continued for more than 50 years until his death on October 21, 1863 at age eighty-one. He donated the Sturgis Library in Barnstable. Sources on Sturgis include *Memoir of the Hon. William Sturgis* (Boston: John Wilson & Sons, 1864), edited by Charles Greely Loring, and *The Journal of William Sturgis: The Eighteenth-Century Memoirs of a Sailor* (Sono Nis, 1978), edited by S.W. Jackman.

One of the last memoirs about the Pacific Northwest maritime fur trade to emerge from the 18th century was by William F. Sturgis who visited the coast at age seventeen.

THE DRAKE CONTROVERSY

Naval historian Edward Von der Porten is one of numerous scholars who have taken objection to R. Samuel Bawlf's *The Secret Voyage of Sir Francis Drake* (2003) which leads one to assume Francis Drake was the first European to reach British Columbia.

"Serious research has long resolved the issues of where Drake traveled in the Pacific," says Von der Porten, president of the Drake Navigators Guild, "and British Columbia could not have been a place he visited. Samuel Bawlf ignores most of the extensive evidence about Francis Drake's visit to the Pacific Coast. His conclusions are fantasies built on speculation derived from hypotheses based on the thinnest of intensively manipulated evidence."

Von der Porten has offered a public rebuttal to *The Secret Voyage of Sir Francis Drake* in which he refutes the notion that Francis Drake could have reached British Columbia "first."

He makes seven points.

• Bawlf brings Drake to the Northwest Coast from Guatulco, Mexico, by using distances in leagues given in the accounts of the voyage. The measurement of the league used by Bawlf is the modern league of 18,228 feet, which would place Drake on the coast of Washington, not Vancouver Island. However, Drake used the Elizabethan league of 15,000 feet, which would put him on the coast in southern Oregon, the latitude accepted by a broad consensus of modern scholars. *Drake never reached the coast of British Columbia.*

• Bawlf states that Drake sailed 2,000 miles in 44 days along the shores of southern Alaska, British Columbia, Washington and Oregon, and made discoveries that later explorers took 20 years to work out. He allows 10 days for stops, leaving 34 days of sailing time. Traveling day and night, his average speed would have had to be 2.45 knots, or 58.8 miles per day. The *Golden Hind* averaged three to four knots in the open ocean in good conditions with favourable winds. Along the shore, Drake could have operated only in daylight.

Allowing for contrary winds and currents, unpredictable tide races, unknown shoals and pinnacle rocks, fog, rain, and all the other vicissitudes of sailing along complex and dangerous unknown coasts and in narrow waterways among islands and peninsulas in one of the coldest years of the Little Ice Age, his average speed could not have reached one knot in daylight—well under 20 miles per day. Bawlf's idea that Drake explored 2,000 miles of the northwest coast in 34 days is impossible.

• Bawlf gives Drake 44 days to explore the coast by accepting the date Drake arrived on the coast which is given in the surviving Elizabethan accounts of the expedition. This is June 3. Bawlf, however, changes the date when Drake ended his exploration and arrived at his Port of *Nova Albion* from June 17 to July 17. Then he changes Drake's departure date from the port from July 23 to August 23. However, Drake visited a group of islands just after leaving his port, according to the accounts, and named them the Isles of Saint James. Saint James' Day is July 25.

So Drake did not leave the islands on August 25 as Bawlf claims, but on July 25. The calendar as given in the contemporary accounts is the correct one. This leaves Drake 14 days—not 44—to carry out his explorations between his arrival on the coast and his

Courtesy of Edward Von der Porten

This portrait by Thomas de Leu depicts Sir Francis Drake at age forty-three, not long after he visited the West Coast of North America.

arrival at the port. With no stops, his day-and-night speed to travel 2,000 miles would have had to be 5.95 knots average, or 142.8 miles per day in a three-to-four-knot ship capable of less than one knot in daylight along an unknown shore. For Drake to explore 2,000 miles of the northwest coast in 14 days—the amount of time he had available to spend on exploration—is impossible.

• The Native-American peoples Drake met were described in great detail in the accounts. Bawlf claims Drake met the peoples who inhabited the shore from southern Alaska to central Oregon: northwest-coast peoples with huge cedar canoes, split-plank communal houses and totems. No such peoples or artifacts are mentioned in the accounts. Ethnographers have shown that the people Drake met at his port were the Coast Miwok People, a California group living at and near latitude 38 degrees north who had a completely different lifestyle from that of the northwest coast peoples. Drake's chroniclers could not have described the costumes, ceremonies, artifacts, words and lifeways of a people they had not seen. Bawlf cannot move a Native-American people north 400 nautical miles.

• Drake's port of *Nova Albion* is given by Bawlf as Whale Cove, Oregon. This site does not have the Native Americans, the prominent white cliffs, the offshore Islands of Saint James, the beach-level fortification location, explorer-period artifacts, an open-bay anchorage adjacent to the sheltered careening port, the characteristics shown in Drake's drawing of the port, a safe location to careen the *Golden Hind*, or reasonable safety of entrance or exit. Whale cove is not even mentioned in the modern *Coast Pilot*. Whale Cove could not have been Drake's port.

• Bawlf ignores most of the evidence in the accounts and early maps and claims those few pieces of evidence he deems "true" have been changed following a series of "rules" created by an Elizabethan conspiracy which he has decoded. Yet the accounts of Drake's voyage have long been shown to be remarkably straightforward, detailed and accurate—notably by English scholar Michael Turner, who has located and confirmed by personal field work more than 95 locations visited by Drake. Bawlf provides no evidence to support his claim of a vast Elizabethan conspiracy.

• Bawlf apparently is not aware of much of the modern research about Drake in the North Pacific, as his bibliography does not mention numerous publications known to most scholars of the field. These publications analyze much evidence that Bawlf does not even mention in his books. Bawlf does not deal with a large body of evidence and analysis about Drake's voyage to the west coast of North America.

Former museum director Edward Von der Porten of San Francisco is President of the Drake Navigators Guild, a non-profit organization that brings together persons from many fields of scholarship to study the early exploration of the west coast of North America.

The search for Francis Drake's California harbour has involved many persons over the span of two centuries. The most intensive research has been organized and conducted by the private, nonprofit Drake Navigators Guild. Since 1949, the Guild has published approximately one thousand pages of research reports analyzing the evidence from the sixteenth century. This research has included work in cartography, geography, ship handling, navigation, hydrography, naval architecture, climatology, botany, zoology, archaeology, ethnography and art history.

The summary of this research is available in a booklet by Raymond Aker and Edward Von der Porten called Discovering Francis Drake's California Harbor *(2000). It contains contributions by Guild members Robert W. Allen, William J. Duddleson, Bruce Keegan, Ernest W. Michelsen, Robert W. Parkinson and Don Thieler.*

It is available for $13 U.S. including postage from 143 Springfield Dr., San Francisco, CA 94132-1456, USA.

Mowachaht hunter wearing sea otter pelts at Nootka Sound (John Webber, 1778).

AFTER THE INVASION

"Unquestionably, the sea-otter trade also had a negative impact on the Northwest Coast Indians. Their health was impaired by alcohol and tobacco and their numbers were reduced by epidemics and fire-arms. It has been estimated that the Indian population of the Northwest Coast fell from about 188,000 in 1774 to about 38,000 in 1874, for an annual decrease of approximately 1.5 per cent (although the population estimates are questionable). Already by 1792 the Nootkas were 'excessively' fond of brandy, wine, and beer, coffee and tea, sweets, bread, and beans. Such dietary deterioration (bread and beans notwithstanding) soon affected the entire coast. Grog promoted sexual promiscuity, which in turn spread venereal disease, which in its own turn caused sterility and death. It was undoubtedly introduced in 1778 at Nootka Sound by Captain Cook's men, who were sexually active wherever they sojourned, especially at Tahiti and Hawaii but also at Nootka and Unalaska (where they found that VD had already been introduced by the Russians). Cook's sailors, like most Euroamerican visitors, found the Nootkan women much less appealing (homelier and dirtier) than their Polynesian sisters, but 'notwithstanding these circumstances, some few of our gentlemen got the better of their feelings, so far as to admit them to their bed, in which case the poor creatures always underwent the ceremony of the mop and pail.' By 1792, the Spaniards noted at Nootka Sound, 'the natives are already beginning to experience the terrible ravages of syphilis.' In 1811 syphilis and consumption (tuberculosis) were the most common afflictions of the Chinooks. Mortality was increased by firearms; by supplementing knives and clubs, guns with their greater firepower made Indian warfare deadlier. Mainly for these reasons the Indian population of Nootka Sound may have dropped from as many as 3,000–4,000 in 1788 to as few as 1,500 in 1804."

—James Gibson, *Otter Skins, Boston Ships, and China Goods: The Maritime Fur Trade of the Northwest Coast, 1785-1841.*

"They look upon paper as a very awful thing, they tremble to see the working of a pen. Writing is, they imagine, a dread mystery. By it the mighty whites seem to carry on intercourse with unseen powers. When they are writing, there's no telling what they may be doing. They may be bidding a pestilence come over the land, or ordering the rain to stay in the west, or giving directions for the salmon to remain in the ocean."

—Reverend Robert Christopher Lundin Brown, *describing some of the origins of the so-called Chilcotin War of 1864.*

2004

Ray Willliams and his wife Terry Williams are the last remaining year-round residents of Yuquot at Nootka Sound, serving as guardians of history for the Nuu-chah-nulth First Nation.

WWW.ABCBOOKWORLD.COM / FIRST NATIONS LITERATURE

For anyone seeking information on books pertaining to First Nations within British Columbia, material is freely available on a reference site generated at www.abcbookworld.com. There are more than 6,500 B.C. authors listed, with biographical and bibliographical information on more than 50 Indian authors and approximately 500 titles about First Nations in B.C. (Search "First Nations Literature," "First Nations," and "Anthropology.")

This site is hosted by Simon Fraser University. As is the case in this text, I have frequently followed the international practice of retaining the word Indian to describe someone who is a member of an indigenous First Nation within Canada, which was the term used in the 18th century.

The word Indian has absurd origins and it is understandably out of fashion with many people, but Native can be problematic and Aboriginal is unduly associated with Australia, although the term Aboriginal is used in the modern Canadian Constitution of 1982. Use of the word Indian herein is not intended to be derogatory or prejudicial. The term British Columbian is equally absurd.